ROBERT G

SELECTED POEMS

ROBERT GRAVES

Selected Poems

edited by Michael Longley

ff

faber and faber

First published in 2013
by Faber and Faber Ltd
Bloomsbury House
74-77 Great Russell Street
London WC1B 3DA

Typeset by RefineCatch Limited, Bungay, Suffolk
Printed in England by T. J. International Ltd, Padstow, Cornwall

A CIP record for this book
is available from the British Library

ISBN 978–0–571–28383–5

FSC
www.fsc.org
MIX
Paper from
responsible sources
FSC® C101712

2 4 6 8 10 9 7 5 3 1

The Patchwork Quilt

Here is this patchwork quilt I've made
Of patterned silks and old brocade,
Small faded rags in memory rich
Sewn each to each with feather stitch,
But if you stare aghast perhaps
At certain muddied khaki scraps
Or trophy-fragments of field grey,
Clotted and torn, a grim display
That never decked white sheets before,
Blame my dazed head, blame bloody war.

Contents

[viii]

Introduction

When Derek Mahon and I were undergraduates at Trinity College Dublin, we inhaled poetry with our Sweet Afton cigarettes. From the beginning Robert Graves emerged as one of our heroes. We read his poems aloud to each other, counting the beats with our hands and scattering cigarette ash into the gully of the 1959 *Collected Poems* (my favourite Graves volume to this day, with our ash lingering as faint smudges between the pages). As a master of the singing line, complex syntax and stanzaic pattern, Graves was an ideal focus for two apprentices. After fifty years, the poems we loved then have lost none of their radiance: they continue to astonish, and are the heartbeat of this selection.

At the same time we were delighting in the louche narratives of Graves's historical novels *I, Claudius* and its sequel *Claudius the God*. Their erotic episodes and insouciant scholarship ensured that these books enjoyed something of a vogue among the repressed Classicists of Trinity College. We shared our copies of the two-volume Penguin *Greek Myths*, and some of us read his other novels, *Wife to Mr Milton*, *King Jesus*, *Homer's Daughter*. For its insights into the nature of poetic experience we turned to *The White Goddess* as a kind of religion substitute, and pilfered its image hoard for our own poems. From the library we borrowed Graves's criticism – *The Common Asphodel*, *The Crowning Privilege*. As a literary critic he was far more lively than anyone we had read before. Mischievous, irreverent, combative, he appealed to our youthful iconoclasm. We cringed guiltily and with masochistic pleasure as he drubbed some of our favourite poets – Yeats, Dylan Thomas – and others we cared for less – Pound and Eliot. Here the debunking outsider is at full throttle:

It is an extraordinary paradox that Pound's ignorant, indecent, unmelodious, seldom metrical Cantos, embellished with esoteric Chinese ideographs – for all I know, they may have been traced from the nearest tea-chest – and with illiterate Greek, Latin, Spanish and Provençal snippets . . . are now compulsory reading in many ancient centres of learning.

Perhaps the prose volume that made the deepest impression was his memoir *Goodbye to All That*, in which Graves revisits the psychic quagmire of the trenches. This awakened my own memories of my father's infrequent reminiscences: he had joined the London Scottish as a boy-soldier in September 1914 and miraculously survived. He was wounded and gassed, and he won the Military Cross. For five decades, in each of my poetry collections, I have been following in his footsteps (and in Graves's). *Goodbye to All That* was not published until 1929. Graves took his time, as did the other major Great War memoirists, Siegfried Sassoon and Edmund Blunden. The terrible subject matter needed time to settle to an adequate imaginative depth. Yes, we hero-worshipped Graves for his astonishing productivity, his enthusiastic learning and independence of mind, his often outrageous and sometimes preposterous opinions, his protean range. But, at an altogether higher altitude, we venerated his poetry. Graves maintained that his prose mountain paid for the inner adventure of poetry: 'Prose books are the show dogs I breed and sell to support my cat.'

*

Not many poets can produce such commanding, resonant, unforgettable opening lines: 'We looked, we loved and therewith instantly / Death became terrible to you and me . . .'; 'All saints revile her, and all sober men / Ruled by the God Apollo's golden mean . . .' I have such lines by heart to this day. Graves lays down the law majestically, and with a chasteness of utterance which, paradoxically, owes something to 'Apollo's golden mean'. Yet his line is flexible, at times improvisatory, jazzy even: 'Never be disenchanted of / That place you sometimes dream yourself into . . .' Or, from 'Mid-Winter Waking': 'O gracious, lofty, shone against from under, / Back-of-the-mind-far clouds like towers.' The metre seems to dissolve in 'blue' notes, the syntax tantalisingly to unravel. In his search for the right word, the vocabulary can become intoxicatingly eccentric, lending the texture of some of his poems a strange brocaded richness. In an early poem, 'Lost Love', we find 'clashing jaws of moth / *Chumbling* holes in cloth . . .' Has 'discontinuance' ever been used in a lyric poem before? It gives a magical lift to the stunning last line of 'The Second-Fated': 'A moon-warmed world of discontinuance.' If the exact word does not exist, Graves will invent it, or (see 'back-of-the-mind-far' above) he will create uncanny compounds. 'The Troll's Nosegay' contains 'Cold fog-drawn Lily, pale mist-magic Rose . . .' In 'The Last Day of Leave' a virtuoso compound comes at the poem's climax: 'blind-fate-aversive afterword'.

This poet is able to take daredevil risks because he has perfect pitch:

> She tells her love while half asleep,
>   In the dark hours,
>   With half-words whispered low:
> As Earth stirs in her winter sleep
>   And puts out grass and flowers
>   Despite the snow,
>   Despite the falling snow.

Between the last two lines there's something akin to a change of key from major to minor (except that the whole poem is in the minor key). The mood floats between keys in a way Chopin would have appreciated. In this and other exquisite lyrics – 'Love Without Hope', 'The Narrow Sea' – Graves is a virtuoso at turning on a sixpence. A connoisseur of riddles and spells and nursery rhymes, he has learned much from the works of Anonymous (and Walter de la Mare):

> Allie, call the children,
>   Call them from the green!
> Allie calls, Allie sings,
>   Soon they run in:
> First there came
> Tom and Madge,
>   Kate and I who'll not forget
> How we played by the water's edge
>   Till the April sun set.

Why is this so heartbreaking? Graves's preternaturally acute ear returns us magically to childhood's half-remembered arcanum. Lewis Carroll or Edward Lear would have been proud to write 'The Untidy Man', an overlooked macabre little gem which I have included here: 'He had rolled his head far underneath the bed: / He had left his legs and arms lying all over the room.' (Might this be a sublimated battlefield memory?) Childhood inspires some of his best known pieces, such as the edgy 'Warning to Children' in which he invokes 'the fewness, muchness, rareness, / Greatness of this endless only / Precious world . . .' and makes it feel like a Pandora's box. 'The Death Room' hits the exact note for the wakefulness and fears of everyone's childhood: '. . . an inconclusive / Circling, spidery, ceiling craquelure, / And, by the window-frame, the well-loathed, lame, / Damp-patch, cross-patch, sleepless L-for-Lemur . . .' Graves can cheerfully free himself from the restraints of the perfected lyric to tell stories ('Welsh

Incident': 'I was coming to that . . .') or indulge his taste for grotesquerie as in 'Ogres and Pygmies': 'They had long beards and stinking arm-pits, / They were wide-mouthed, long-yarded and great-bellied . . .' As a rule, the rhythm is consummately pitched, however free-wheeling the lines.

*

Robert Graves was born in London in 1895 of mixed 'Irish-Scottish-Danish-German' parentage. His father, Alfred Perceval Graves, himself a poet, was Irish. His mother was German and related to the historian Leopold von Ranke. Through two world wars Graves's German connections were such an embarrassment that he protected himself by insisting on his Irish paternity. (In the Foreword to his *Collected Poems 1959* he writes that his poems 'remain true to the Anglo-Irish poetic tradition into which I was born'.) He attended a succession of preparatory schools where he learned to 'keep a straight bat at cricket, and to have a high moral sense'. His public school was Charterhouse, which he found 'conventional, hypocritical and anti-intellectual'. Graves left school a week before the outbreak of war in 1914, and joined the Royal Welch Fusiliers as an officer. He served in France from 1915, and fought at the Battle of Loos and the Battle of the Somme. Of Graves's school generation one in three died in the war. On his twenty-first birthday he was himself reported killed in action and letters of condolence were dispatched. Though he detested the officer caste, he always respected courage and soldierly values. More than was the case with the other war poets (an exception being Ivor Gurney of the Gloucestershires), he professed an open-faced, almost naïve regimental loyalty. His attitude and tone were not necessarily those which we associate with 'protest poetry': 'I like feeling really frightened and if happiness consists in being miserable in a good cause, why then I'm doubly happy.' Being a 'jolly young Fusilier' mattered deeply to Graves; and at his memorial service in

London in December 1985 'The Last Post' was played by a Royal Welch Fusilier.

In *Goodbye to All That* the prose sometimes approaches the condition of poetry, as in this description of No Man's Land:

> I looked at the German trenches through a periscope – a distant streak of sandbags . . . The enemy gave no sign, except for a wisp or two of wood-smoke where they, too, were boiling up a hot drink. Between us and them lay a flat meadow with cornflowers, marguerites and poppies growing in the long grass, a few shell holes, the bushes I had seen the night before, the wreck of an aeroplane, our barbed wire and theirs. Three-quarters of a mile away stood a big ruined house; a quarter of a mile behind that, a red-brick village – Auchy – poplars and haystacks, a tall chimney, and another village – Haisnes. Half-right, pit-head and smaller slag heaps. La Bassée lay half-left; the sun caught the weather-vane of the church and made it twinkle.

Graves wrote several exceptional war poems which his older self ignored or suppressed ('The Patchwork Quilt', the touching poem which I have placed as an epigraph to this selection, was never published). Perhaps the future devotee of the White Goddess regretted their homoeroticism. Perhaps he feared that they compared unfavourably with the war poems of Siegfried Sassoon and Wilfred Owen. He enjoyed a bumpy friendship with Sassoon, to whom 'Two Fusiliers' is addressed. And Graves pleaded loyally on his behalf when Sassoon made his famous declaration against the prolongation of the war. He probably saved Sassoon from court-martial and prison by arranging to have him admitted as a neurasthenic patient at Craiglockhart Hospital outside Edinburgh. There Sassoon met

Wilfred Owen, as did Graves when he visited Sassoon. The poets read and absorbed each other's poems. In the history of English poetry this was a momentous coincidence of talent, with Graves a crucial part of it. Graves is among the poets of the Great War commemorated on the stone in Poets' Corner in Westminster Abbey. His strongest war poems deserve to be read alongside those of his peers. 'A Dead Boche' shocks like a harrowing war photograph: '. . . he scowled and stunk / With clothes and face a sodden green'.

Some of Graves's war poems were written in retrospect. Published in 1925, 'A Letter from Wales' is a rich, complex, informally cadenced meditation on war and friendship, on death, identity and poetry; it ends with the *cri de cœur*: 'How am I to put / The question that I'm asking you to answer?' In 'Recalling War' (included in *Collected Poems*, 1938) Graves reviews the ghastly waste: 'War was return of earth to ugly earth, / War was foundering of sublimities, / Extinction of each happy art and faith / By which the world had still kept head in air.' Again, but this time with no grandiloquence, 'The Last Day of Leave' (subtitled '1916' and collected in 1948) suggests the horror in a beautifully understated drama:

> But when it [the sun] rolled down level with us,
> Four pairs of eyes sought mine as if appealing
> For a blind-fate-aversive afterword –
>
> 'Do you remember the lily lake?
> We were all there, all five of us in love,
> Not one yet killed, widowed or broken-hearted.'

In *The Great War and Modern Memory* Paul Fussell, discussing what he calls 'The British Homoerotic Tradition', touches on 'the unique physical tenderness, the readiness to admire openly the bodily beauty of young men, the unapologetic recognition that men may be in love with each other.' He quotes Graves's 'sensuous little ode', 'Not Dead', written to the memory of David Thomas, a young man loved by both Sassoon and Graves, in what Graves considered his transient public-school homosexual phase ('pseudo-homosexual', as he put it): 'Walking through trees to cool my heat and pain, / I know that David's with me here again.' The last lines are: 'Over the whole wood in a little while / Breaks his slow smile.' John Keegan ends his great history *The First World War* with this profound meditation:

> Comradeship flourished in the earthwork cities of the Western and Eastern Fronts, bound strangers into the closest brotherhood, elevated the loyalties created within the ethos of temporary regimentality to the status of life-and-death blood ties. Men whom the trenches cast into intimacy entered into bonds of mutual dependency and sacrifice of self stronger than any of the friendships made in peace and better times. That is the ultimate mystery of the First World War. If we could understand its loves, as well as its hates, we would be nearer understanding the mystery of human life.

Although he did not like to be called a war poet, the story of Great War poetry is incomplete without the war poems of Robert Graves. His war poems are love poems in their way.

*

Home on leave before the armistice, Graves married the artist Nancy Nicholson, daughter of William Nicholson, the painter. They had four children. After the war he briefly attended St John's College, Oxford. In his thesis for a B.Litt, published as *Poetic Unreason*, he argues that there is in poetry a 'supralogical element' and that the 'latent associations' of the words used in a poem often contradict its prose sense. He was, again briefly, Professor of English at Cairo (on the recommendation of T. E. Lawrence). The war left Graves shell-shocked, mentally scarred for many years: '. . . the fear of gas obsessed me: any unusual smell, even a strong smell of flowers in a garden, was enough to set me trembling . . . the noise of a car back-firing would send me flat on my face, or running for cover.' His marriage failed, and in 1926 he left his wife and four children to live in Majorca with the American poet Laura Riding. They collaborated as critics on such books as *A Survey of Modernist Poetry* and *A Pamphlet Against Anthologies*. They founded the Seizin Press and published a select list of finely produced books and the critical miscellany *Epilogue*. Riding's megalomaniac personality, powerful intellect and uncompromising theories overwhelmed Graves. He was in thrall. In her sympathetic biography *Life on the Edge* Miranda Seymour describes the relationship:

> From now on, he dedicated himself to protecting her reputation, honouring her with gifts, and showing an unquestioning deference to her wishes . . . Riding's inflexible certainty about what was right and what was wrong provided him with values in which he could trust. He honestly believed that her supervision was making him into a better – because a more honest – writer.

In his study *Swifter Than Reason: The Poetry and Criticism of Robert Graves*, Douglas Day asserts: 'The influence of Laura Riding is quite possibly the most important single element in his poetic career.' This goes too far, but Day is right to add that 'some of his best work was done during the years of his literary partnership with Laura Riding'. In 1939 she ended the bizarre alliance that had lasted for thirteen tumultuous years. Graves continued to admire her – 'a perfect original'. She had helped him to concentrate his lyric power, and she inspired some fine love poems. But Laura Riding had also exhausted him. He now needed to compose himself, to quieten down.

He married Beryl Hodge, formerly the wife of one of his collaborators Alan Hodge, and in 1946 returned with her and their children (they eventually had four) to live in Deyá in Majorca where, apart from occasional forays to England and America to give lectures, he remained for the rest of his life. This was a fruitful time for Graves and, in addition to distinguished prose, he wrote some of his finest poems: 'Mid-Winter Waking' ('Stirring suddenly from long hibernation, / I knew myself once more a poet . . .'); 'Theseus and Ariadne' ('High on his figured couch beyond the waves / He dreams ...') Might the first of these be an oblique reproach to Laura's ferocious domination, and an expression of gratitude for Beryl's 'sudden warm airs'? In 1961 he was elected Professor of Poetry at Oxford in succession to W. H. Auden; and in 1968 he was awarded the Queen's Gold Medal for Poetry.

*

Love poems such as 'With Her Lips Only', 'A Former Attachment', 'Pure Death', 'Never Such Love', 'The Thieves', 'Through Nightmare' will live as long as the language lives. They are irradiated, of course, by sexual desire but also by Graves's investigations for *The White Goddess*. In 1948 he completed this 'historical grammar of poetic myth', which Richard Ellmann calls 'a matriarchal study of history, personality and poetic inspiration'. This idiosyncratic amalgam of studious survey and imaginative surmise resembles Yeats's *A Vision* which, Yeats said, gave him 'metaphors for poetry'. In the introduction to *Graves and the Goddess* Ian Firla and Grevel Lindop write: 'Neglected by most academic scholars of modern poetry, alternately celebrated and reviled by feminists, banished from the syllabus in departments of classics, Celtic studies, and anthropology, *The White Goddess* has nonetheless exerted a persistent influence in these and many other fields for more than half a century and has continued, above all, to be a central source of inspiration for poets, the more potent for remaining hidden.' They quote Keith Sagar: 'The single most important influence which Ted Hughes offered to the intellectual development of Sylvia Plath as their relationship began in 1956 was a fully worked-out belief in the poetic mythology of Robert Graves's *The White Goddess*.'

So, what is it all about? In the first chapter Graves explains:

> The theme, briefly, is the antique story . . . of the birth, life, death and resurrection of the God of the Waxing Year; the central chapters concern the God's losing battle with the God of the Waning Year for love of the capricious and all-powerful Threefold Goddess, their mother, bride and layer-out. The poet identifies himself with the God of the Waxing Year and his Muse with the Goddess; the rival is his blood-brother, his other self, his weird. All true poetry . . . celebrates some incident or scene in this very ancient story, and the three main characters are so much a part of our racial inheritance that they not only assert themselves in poetry but recur on occasions of emotional stress in the form of dreams, paranoiac visions and delusions.

Many of Graves's finest poems are rooted in this vast, multifaceted compendium with its ogham stones, sacred animals and magic trees, its backdrop of Greek and Celtic, Hebraic and Egyptian mythologies. 'To Juan at the Winter Solstice' links, in a rosary of seven stanzas, themes and images from the book. Here is the penultimate stanza, lines heavily freighted and yet exquisitely melodious:

Much snow is falling, winds roar hollowly,
The owl hoots from the elder,
Fear in your heart cries to the loving-cup:
Sorrow to sorrow as the sparks fly upward.
The log groans and confesses:
There is one story and one story only.

In his *Third Book of Criticism* Randall Jarrell sums up Graves's devotion to the White Goddess. Affectionate and amused though it may be, this essay annoyed Graves:

> All that is finally important to Graves is condensed in the one figure of the Mother-Mistress-Muse, she who creates, nourishes, seduces, destroys; she who saves us – or, as good as saving, destroys us – as long as we love her, write poems to her, submit to her without question, use all our professional, Regimental, masculine qualities in her service. Death is swallowed up in victory, said St Paul; for Graves Life, Death, everything that exists is swallowed up in the White Goddess.

Graves himself could put it very simply: 'A Muse-poet falls in love, absolutely, and his true love is for him the embodiment of the Muse.' Or, yet again: 'There is one story and one story only / That will prove worth your telling.'

*

'Where are poems? Why do I now write none?' Graves laments in the late poem 'At the Gate'. 'Where have my ancient powers suddenly gone?' In his old age Graves, in Paul O'Prey's words, 'attempted to maintain his poetic gifts by consciously exposing himself to the vicissitudes of romantic love; between 1950 and 1974 he "experienced" the Goddess through four different "muse-possessed" women.' Beryl must have been a very tolerant wife.

In the introduction to his finely judged *Selected Poems* of 1985 O'Prey, who knew Graves well, writes:

> Unfortunately, when the time came to edit the 1975 edition of the *Collected Poems*, Graves, by then in his eighties, felt he could no longer trust his own judgement so decided to publish *all* the later poems; this not only made the book 'top-heavy' but meant that the 'real poems', as he calls them, were obscured among the rather large quantity of 'mistakes and digressions'.

By and large I have followed O'Prey's 'decluttering'. In many of the later poems Graves seems to be flying on automatic pilot; the lines go clickety-click like a Rubik's Cube; the rhythmic resolutions fail to cover up emotional gaps and flimsy argument. He blurs the focus of *The White Goddess* and reduces this (for him) religious text to a highfalutin rigmarole that can sometimes look like an alibi for an old poet's philandering with younger women. The results can be tiresome and embarrassing. 'How It Started' concerns 'a wild midnight dance, in my own garden': 'In the circumstances I stayed away / Until you fetched me out on the tiled floor / Where, acting as an honorary teenager, / I kicked off both my shoes.' But even in the doldrums of his final phase gusts of inspiration blow, as in 'Three Times in Love' ('You have now fallen three times in love / With the same woman . . .'); and 'Crucibles of Love' in which Graves in his old age continues to ask leading questions: 'From where do poems come?'

*

'Since the age of fifteen poetry has been my ruling passion and I have never intentionally undertaken any task or formed any relationship that seemed inconsistent with poetic principles; which has sometimes won me the reputation of an eccentric.' In his single-minded devotion to his poetic vocation and the fortitude it required of him, Graves most resembles W. B. Yeats. They could both be preposterous. But, to borrow Auden's line from his elegy for Yeats: 'You were silly like us: your gift survived it all.' I first read Graves in *The Penguin Book of Contemporary Verse* (1950). Kenneth Allott's clear-headed opinion in the prefatory note to his generous selection still seems spot-on: 'The poetry of Robert Graves is in some ways the purest poetry produced in our time, waving no flags, addressed to no congregation, designed neither to comfort nor to persuade. It is poetry with roots in everyday experience, but it always has the quality of making that experience new, pungent, and exciting.'

Graves's influence is multifarious. If *The White Goddess* (perhaps disturbingly) impressed Hughes and Plath, Graves influenced Philip Larkin and the so-called 'Movement' poets in other ways. In *The Movement*, his study of English poetry and fiction of the 1950s, Blake Morrison writes: 'Though all the Movement looked to Graves as a poet who had shown the possibilities inherent in a non-Modernist tradition, different members of the group responded to different qualities in his work.' Philip Larkin had his own slant. Reviewing *Steps* in the *Manchester Guardian* in 1958, he is somewhat agnostic but ultimately affirming: 'Neither respectful nor vulgar, unlettered nor pedantic, unbalanced nor entirely sane, Mr Graves is as good a poetic mentor as the young are likely to get.' My two favourite titles for 'poet' are the Scots word *makar* and Horace's *musarum sacerdos*, 'priest of the Muses'. Again and again Robert Graves brilliantly succeeds in uniting craft and vision:

> We spell away the overhanging night,
> We spell away the soldiers and the fright.

Michael Longley
Belfast
June 2012

Editorial Note

All the poems selected here can be found in *The Complete Poems* edited by Beryl Graves and Dunstan Ward. This magisterial work was originally published by Carcanet Press, first in three volumes, then in one, and subsequently by Penguin Books in their Modern Classics series. I am deeply indebted to Dunstan Ward for making available the text of the poems as printed in that edition. I have followed the chronological order adopted by him and Beryl Graves, from *Over the Brazier* (1916) to *Collected Poems 1975*. Their great collection concludes with two sections, *Uncollected Poems (1910–1974)* and *Unpublished and Posthumously Published Poems*. From the first I have selected 'Bazentin, 1916', 'The Untidy Man' and 'Assumption Day'; from the second, 'Return'. I have restored these four poems to their chronological home towards the beginning of this book. William Graves's devotedly edited compilation of his father's war poems, *Poems About War* (Moyer Bell Limited, 1988), has been an inspiration. The beautiful lyric 'The Patchwork Quilt', which dates from July 1918, would have been lost were it not for his vigilance. It moves me to print it here as the epigraph to my selection. Detailed advice has been generously given by Fran Brearton and Peter McDonald, two sagacious Gravesians. I also thank Ronald Ewart and Edna Longley for their valuable support.

M. L.

ROBERT GRAVES

Selected Poems

In the Wilderness

He, of his gentleness,
Thirsting and hungering
Walked in the wilderness;
Soft words of grace he spoke
Unto lost desert-folk
That listened wondering.
He heard the bittern call
From ruined palace-wall,
Answered him brotherly;
He held communion
With the she-pelican
Of lonely piety.
Basilisk, cockatrice,
Flocked to his homilies,
With mail of dread device,
With monstrous barbèd stings,
With eager dragon-eyes;
Great bats on leathern wings
And old, blind, broken things
Mean in their miseries.
Then ever with him went,
Of all his wanderings
Comrade, with ragged coat,
Gaunt ribs – poor innocent –
Bleeding foot, burning throat,
The guileless young scapegoat:
For forty nights and days
Followed in Jesus' ways,
Sure guard behind him kept,
Tears like a lover wept.

I've watched the Seasons passing slow, so slow,
In the fields between La Bassée and Béthune;
Primroses and the first warm day of Spring,
Red poppy floods of June,
August, and yellowing Autumn, so
To Winter nights knee-deep in mud or snow,
And you've been everything,

Dear, you've been everything that I most lack
In these soul-deadening trenches – pictures, books,
Music, the quiet of an English wood,
Beautiful comrade-looks,
The narrow, bouldered mountain-track,
The broad, full-bosomed ocean, green and black,
And Peace, and all that's good.

Goliath and David

*(For Lieut. David Thomas, 1st Batt. Royal Welch
Fusiliers, killed at Fricourt, March, 1916)*

'If I am Jesse's son,' said he,
'Where must that tall Goliath be?'
For once an earlier David took
Smooth pebbles from the brook:
Out between the lines he went
To that one-sided tournament,
A shepherd boy who stood out fine
And young to fight a Philistine
Clad all in brazen mail. He swears
That he's killed lions, he's killed bears,

And those that scorn the God of Zion
Shall perish so like bear or lion.
But . . . the historian of that fight
Had not the heart to tell it right.

Striding within javelin range,
Goliath marvels at this strange
Goodly-faced boy so proud of strength.
David's clear eye measures the length;
With hand thrust back, he cramps one knee,
Poises a moment thoughtfully,
And hurls with a long vengeful swing.
The pebble, humming from the sling
Like a wild bee, flies a sure line
For the forehead of the Philistine;
Then . . . but there comes a brazen clink,
And quicker than a man can think
Goliath's shield parries each cast,
Clang! clang! And clang! was David's last.

Scorn blazes in the Giant's eye,
Towering unhurt six cubits high.
Says foolish David, 'Curse your shield!
And curse my sling! but I'll not yield.'
He takes his staff of Mamre oak,
A knotted shepherd-staff that's broke
The skull of many a wolf and fox
Come filching lambs from Jesse's flocks.
Loud laughs Goliath, and that laugh
Can scatter chariots like blown chaff
To rout; but David, calm and brave,
Holds his ground, for God will save.
Steel crosses wood, a flash, and oh!
Shame for beauty's overthrow!
(God's eyes are dim, His ears are shut),

One cruel backhand sabre-cut –
'I'm hit! I'm killed!' young David cries,
Throws blindly forward, chokes . . . and dies.
Steel-helmeted and grey and grim
Goliath straddles over him.

A Dead Boche

To you who'd read my songs of War
    And only hear of blood and fame,
I'll say (you've heard it said before)
    'War's Hell!' and if you doubt the same,
To-day I found in Mametz Wood
A certain cure for lust of blood:

Where, propped against a shattered trunk,
    In a great mess of things unclean,
Sat a dead Boche; he scowled and stunk
    With clothes and face a sodden green,
Big-bellied, spectacled, crop-haired,
Dribbling black blood from nose and beard.

Not Dead

Walking through trees to cool my heat and pain,
I know that David's with me here again.
All that is simple, happy, strong, he is.
Caressingly I stroke
Rough bark of the friendly oak.
A brook goes bubbling by: the voice is his.
Turf burns with pleasant smoke;

I laugh at chaffinch and at primroses.
All that is simple, happy, strong, he is.
Over the whole wood in a little while
Breaks his slow smile.

The Legion

'Is that the Three-and-Twentieth, Strabo mine,
Marching below, and we still gulping wine?'
From the sad magic of his fragrant cup
The red-faced old centurion started up,
Cursed, battered on the table. 'No,' he said,
'Not that! The Three-and-Twentieth Legion's dead,
Dead in the first year of this damned campaign –
The Legion's dead, dead, and won't rise again.
Pity? Rome pities her brave lads that die,
But we need pity also, you and I,
Whom Gallic spear and Belgian arrow miss,
Who live to see the Legion come to this:
Unsoldierlike, slovenly, bent on loot,
Grumblers, diseased, unskilled to thrust or shoot.
O brown cheek, muscled shoulder, sturdy thigh!
Where are they now? God! watch it straggle by,
The sullen pack of ragged, ugly swine!
Is that the Legion, Gracchus? Quick, the wine!'
'Strabo,' said Gracchus, 'you are strange to-night.
The Legion is the Legion, it's all right.
If these new men are slovenly, in your thinking,
Hell take it! you'll not better them by drinking.
They all try, Strabo; trust their hearts and hands.
The Legion is the Legion while Rome stands,
And these same men before the autumn's fall
Shall bang old Vercingetorix out of Gaul.'

Two Fusiliers

And have we done with War at last?
Well, we've been lucky devils both,
And there's no need of pledge or oath
To bind our lovely friendship fast,
By firmer stuff
Close bound enough.

By wire and wood and stake we're bound,
By Fricourt and by Festubert,
By whipping rain, by the sun's glare,
By all the misery and loud sound,
By a Spring day,
By Picard clay.

Show me the two so closely bound
As we, by the wet bond of blood,
By friendship blossoming from mud,
By Death: we faced him, and we found
Beauty in Death,
In dead men, breath.

To R. N.

*(From Frise on the Somme in February 1917,
in answer to a letter, saying: 'I am just finishing
my "Faun" poem: I wish you were here
to feed him with cherries.')*

Here by a snow-bound river
In scrapen holes we shiver,
And like old bitterns we
Boom to you plaintively;

[8]

Robert, how can I rhyme
Verses at your desire –
Sleek fauns and cherry-time,
Vague music and green trees,
Hot sun and gentle breeze,
England in June attire,
And life born young again,
For your gay goatish brute
Drunk with warm melody
Singing on beds of thyme
With red and rolling eye,
Waking with wanton lute
All the Devonian plain,
Lips dark with juicy stain,
Ears hung with bobbing fruit?
Why should I keep him time?
Why in this cold and rime,
Where even to dream is pain?
No, Robert, there's no reason;
Cherries are out of season,
Ice grips at branch and root,
And singing birds are mute.

Bazentin, 1916

(A Reminiscence – Robert and David)

R. That was a curious night two years ago,
   Relieving those tired Dockers at Bazentin.
   Remember climbing up between the ruins?
   The guide that lost his head when the gas-shells came,
   Lurching about this way and that, half-witted,
   Till we were forced to find the way ourselves?

D. Yes, twilight torn with flashes, faces muffled,
   In stinking masks, and eyes all sore and crying
   With lachrymatory stuff, and four men gassed.

R. Yet we got up there safely, found the trenches
   Untraversed shallow ditches, along a road
   With dead men sprawled about, some ours,
       some theirs.

D. Ours mostly, and those Dockers doing nothing,
   Tired out, poor devils: much too tired to dig,
   Or to do anything but just hold the ground:
   No touch on either flank, no touch in front,
   Everything in the air. I cursed, I tell you.
   Out went the Dockers, quick as we filed in,
   And soon we'd settled down and put things
       straight,
   Posted the guns, dug in, got out patrols,
   And sent to right and left to restore touch.

R. There was a sunken road out on the right,
   With rifle-pits half dug; at every pit
   A dead man had his head thrust in for shelter.

D. Dawn found us happy enough; a funny day –
   The strangest I remember in all those weeks.
   German five-nines were bracketing down our
       trenches
   Morning and afternoon.

R.   Why, yes; at dinner,
   Three times my cup was shaken out of my hand
   And filled with dirt: I had to pour out fresh.

D. That was the mug you took from the Boche gun.
   Remember that field gun, with the team killed
   By a lucky shot just as the German gunners

Were limbering up? We found the gunner's
    treasures
In a box behind, his lump of fine white chalk
Carefully carved, and painted with a message
Of love to his dear wife, and Allied flags,
A list of German victories, and an eagle.
Then his clean washing, and his souvenirs –
British shell-heads, French bullets, lumps of
    shrapnel,
Nothing much more. I never thought it lucky
To take that sort of stuff.

R.   Then a tame magpie –
German, we guessed – came hopping into the trench,
Picking up scraps of food. That's 'One for sorrow'
I said to little Owen.

D.   Not much mistaken
In the event, when only three days later
They threw us at High Wood and (mind, we got
    there!)
Smashed up the best battalion in the whole corps.
But, Robert, quite the queerest thing that day
Happened in the late afternoon. Worn out,
I snatched two hours of sleep; the Boche
    bombardment
Roared on, but I commended my soul to God,
And slept half through it; but as I lay there snoring
A mouse, in terror of all these wild alarms,
Crept down my neck for shelter, and woke me up
In a great sweat. Blindly I gave one punch
And slew the rascal at the small of my back.
That was a strange day!

R.   Yes, and a merry one.

Assumption Day

What was wrong with the day, doubtless,
Was less the unseasonable gusty weather
Than the bells ringing on a Monday morning
For a church-feast that nobody could welcome –
Not even the bell-ringers.

The pond had shrunk: its yellow lilies
Poked rubbery necks out of the water.
I paused and sat down crossly on a tussock,
My back turned on the idle water-beetles
That would not skim, but floated.

A wasp, a humble-bee, a blue-fly
Uncoöperatively at work together
Were sucking honey from the crowded blossom
Of a pale flower whose name someone once told me –
Someone to be mistrusted.

But, not far off, our little cow-herd
Made mud-cakes, with one eye on the cattle,
And marked each separate cake with his initials.
I was half-tempted by the child's example
To rescue my spoilt morning.

Return

'Farewell,' the Corporal cried, 'La Bassée trenches!
No Cambrins for me now, no more Givenchies,
And no more bloody brickstacks – God Almighty,
I'm back again at last to dear old Blighty.'

But cushy wounds don't last a man too long,
And now, poor lad, he sings this bitter song:
'Back to La Bassée, to the same old hell,
Givenchy, Cuinchey, Cambrin, Loos, Vermelles.'

Corporal Stare

Back from the line one night in June,
I gave a dinner at Béthune –
Seven courses, the most gorgeous meal
Money could buy or batman steal.
Five hungry lads welcomed the fish
With shouts that nearly cracked the dish;
Asparagus came with tender tops,
Strawberries in cream, and mutton chops.
Said Jenkins, as my hand he shook,
'They'll put this in the history book.'
We bawled Church anthems *in choro*
Of Bethlehem and Hermon snow,
With drinking-songs, a mighty sound
To help the good red Pommard round.
Stories and laughter interspersed,
We drowned a long La Bassée thirst –
Trenches in June make throats damned dry.
Then through the window suddenly,
Badge, stripes and medals all complete,
We saw him swagger up the street,
Just like a live man – Corporal Stare!
Stare! Killed last month at Festubert,
Caught on patrol near the Boche wire,
Torn horribly by machine-gun fire!
He paused, saluted smartly, grinned,
Then passed away like a puff of wind,

Leaving us blank astonishment.
The song broke, up we started, leant
Out of the window – nothing there,
Not the least shadow of Corporal Stare,
Only a quiver of smoke that showed
A fag-end dropped on the silent road.

Lost Love

His eyes are quickened so with grief,
He can watch a grass or leaf
Every instant grow; he can
Clearly through a flint wall see,
Or watch the startled spirit flee
From the throat of a dead man.
   Across two counties he can hear
And catch your words before you speak.
The woodlouse or the maggot's weak
Clamour rings in his sad ear,
And noise so slight it would surpass
Credence – drinking sound of grass,
Worm talk, clashing jaws of moth
Chumbling holes in cloth;
The groan of ants who undertake
Gigantic loads for honour's sake
(Their sinews creak, their breath comes thin);
Whir of spiders when they spin,
And minute whispering, mumbling, sighs
Of idle grubs and flies.
   This man is quickened so with grief,
He wanders god-like or like thief
Inside and out, below, above,
Without relief seeking lost love.

[14]

One Hard Look

Small gnats that fly
In hot July
And lodge in sleeping ears,
Can rouse therein
A trumpet's din
With Day of Judgement fears.

Small mice at night
Can wake more fright
Than lions at midday;
A straw will crack
The camel's back –
There is no easier way.

One smile relieves
A heart that grieves
Though deadly sad it be,
And one hard look
Can close the book
That lovers love to see.

Rocky Acres

This is a wild land, country of my choice,
With harsh craggy mountain, moor ample and bare.
Seldom in these acres is heard any voice
But voice of cold water that runs here and there
Through rocks and lank heather growing without care.
No mice in the heath run, no song-birds fly
For fear of the buzzard that floats in the sky.

He soars and he hovers, rocking on his wings,
He scans his wide parish with a sharp eye,
He catches the trembling of small hidden things,
He tears them in pieces, dropping them from the sky;
Tenderness and pity the heart will deny,
Where life is but nourished by water and rock –
A hardy adventure, full of fear and shock.

Time has never journeyed to this lost land,
Crakeberry and heather bloom out of date,
The rocks jut, the streams flow singing on either hand,
Careless if the season be early or late,
The skies wander overhead, now blue, now slate;
Winter would be known by his cutting snow
If June did not borrow his armour also.

Yet this is my country, beloved by me best,
The first land that rose from Chaos and the Flood,
Nursing no valleys for comfort or rest,
Trampled by no shod hooves, bought with no blood.
Sempiternal country whose barrows have stood
Stronghold for demigods when on earth they go,
Terror for fat burghers on far plains below.

Allie

Allie, call the birds in,
   The birds from the sky!
Allie calls, Allie sings,
   Down they all fly:
First there came
Two white doves,
   Then a sparrow from his nest,
Then a clucking bantam hen,
   Then a robin red-breast.

Allie, call the beasts in,
  The beasts, every one!
Allie calls, Allie sings,
  In they all run:
First there came
Two black lambs,
  Then a grunting Berkshire sow,
Then a dog without a tail,
  Then a red and white cow.

Allie, call the fish up,
  The fish from the stream!
Allie calls, Allie sings,
  Up they all swim:
First there came
Two gold fish,
  A minnow and a miller's thumb,
Then a school of little trout,
  Then the twisting eels come.

Allie, call the children,
  Call them from the green!
Allie calls, Allie sings,
  Soon they run in:
First there came
Tom and Madge,
  Kate and I who'll not forget
How we played by the water's edge
  Till the April sun set.

The Untidy Man

There was a man, a very untidy man,
   Whose fingers could nowhere be found to put in his tomb.
He had rolled his head far underneath the bed:
   He had left his legs and arms lying all over the room.

Outlaws

Owls – they whinny down the night;
   Bats go zigzag by.
Ambushed in shadow beyond sight
   The outlaws lie.

Old gods, tamed to silence, there
   In the wet woods they lurk,
Greedy of human stuff to snare
   In nets of murk.

Look up, else your eye will drown
   In a moving sea of black;
Between the tree-tops, upside down,
   Goes the sky-track.

Look up, else your feet will stray
   Into that ambuscade
Where spider-like they trap their prey
   With webs of shade.

For though creeds whirl away in dust,
   Faith dies and men forget,
These agèd gods of power and lust
   Cling to life yet –

Old gods almost dead, malign,
  Starving for unpaid dues:
Incense and fire, salt, blood and wine
  And a drumming muse,

Banished to woods and a sickly moon,
  Shrunk to mere bogey things,
Who spoke with thunder once at noon
  To prostrate kings:

With thunder from an open sky
  To warrior, virgin, priest,
Bowing in fear with a dazzled eye
  Toward the dread East –

Proud gods, humbled, sunk so low,
  Living with ghosts and ghouls,
And ghosts of ghosts and last year's snow
  And dead toadstools.

Haunted

Gulp down your wine, old friends of mine,
Roar through the darkness, stamp and sing
And lay ghost hands on everything,
But leave the noonday's warm sunshine
To living lads for mirth and wine.

I meet you suddenly down the street,
Strangers assume your phantom faces,
You grin at me from daylight places,
Dead, long dead, I'm ashamed to greet
Dead men down the morning street.

The Troll's Nosegay

A simple nosegay! was that much to ask?
(Winter still nagged, with scarce a bud yet showing.)
He loved her ill, if he resigned the task.
'Somewhere,' she cried, 'there must be blossom blowing.'
It seems my lady wept and the troll swore
By Heaven he hated tears: he'd cure her spleen –
Where she had begged one flower he'd shower fourscore,
A bunch fit to amaze a China Queen.

Cold fog-drawn Lily, pale mist-magic Rose
He conjured, and in a glassy cauldron set
With elvish unsubstantial Mignonette
And such vague bloom as wandering dreams enclose.
But she?
    Awed,
        Charmed to tears,
                Distracted,
                        Yet –
Even yet, perhaps, a trifle piqued – who knows?

The Pier-Glass

Lost manor where I walk continually
A ghost, though yet in woman's flesh and blood.
Up your broad stairs mounting with outspread fingers
And gliding steadfast down your corridors
I come by nightly custom to this room,
And even on sultry afternoons I come
Drawn by a thread of time-sunk memory.

Empty, unless for a huge bed of state
Shrouded with rusty curtains drooped awry
(A puppet theatre where malignant fancy
Peoples the wings with fear). At my right hand
A ravelled bell-pull hangs in readiness
To summon me from attic glooms above
Service of elder ghosts; here, at my left,
A sullen pier-glass, cracked from side to side,
Scorns to present the face (as do new mirrors)
With a lying flush, but shows it melancholy
And pale, as faces grow that look in mirrors.

Is there no life, nothing but the thin shadow
And blank foreboding, never a wainscot rat
Rasping a crust? Or at the window-pane
No fly, no bluebottle, no starveling spider?
The windows frame a prospect of cold skies
Half-merged with sea, as at the first creation –
Abstract, confusing welter. Face about,
Peer rather in the glass once more, take note
Of self, the grey lips and long hair dishevelled,
Sleep-staring eyes. Ah, mirror, for Christ's love
Give me one token that there still abides
Remote – beyond this island mystery,
So be it only this side Hope, somewhere,
In streams, on sun-warm mountain pasturage –
True life, natural breath; not this phantasma.

Love in Barrenness

Below the ridge a raven flew
And we heard the lost curlew
Mourning out of sight below.

[21]

Mountain tops were touched with snow;
Even the long dividing plain
Showed no wealth of sheep or grain,
But fields of boulders lay like corn
And raven's croak was shepherd's horn
Where slow cloud-shadow strayed across
A pasture of thin heath and moss.

The North Wind rose: I saw him press
With lusty force against your dress,
Moulding your body's inward grace
And streaming off from your set face;
So now no longer flesh and blood
But poised in marble flight you stood.
O wingless Victory, loved of men,
Who could withstand your beauty then?

Angry Samson

Are they blind, the lords of Gaza
  In their strong towers,
Who declare Samson pillow-smothered
  And stripped of his powers?

O stolid Philistines,
  Stare now in amaze
At my foxes running in your cornfields
  With their tails ablaze,

At swung jaw-bone, at bees swarming
  In the stark lion's hide,
At these, the gates of well-walled Gaza
  A-clank to my stride.

An English Wood

This valley wood is pledged
To the set shape of things,
And reasonably hedged:
Here are no harpies fledged,
No rocs may clap their wings,
Nor gryphons wave their stings.
Here, poised in quietude,
Calm elementals brood
On the set shape of things:
They fend away alarms
From this green wood.
Here nothing is that harms –
No bulls with lungs of brass,
No toothed or spiny grass,
No tree whose clutching arms
Drink blood when travellers pass,
No mount of glass;
No bardic tongues unfold
Satires or charms.
Only, the lawns are soft,
The tree-stems, grave and old;
Slow branches sway aloft,
The evening air comes cold,
The sunset scatters gold.
Small grasses toss and bend,
Small pathways idly tend
Towards no fearful end.

Full Moon

As I walked out that sultry night,
   I heard the stroke of One.
The moon, attained to her full height,
   Stood beaming like the sun:
She exorcized the ghostly wheat
To mute assent in love's defeat,
   Whose tryst had now begun.

The fields lay sick beneath my tread,
   A tedious owlet cried,
A nightingale above my head
   With this or that replied –
Like man and wife who nightly keep
Inconsequent debate in sleep
   As they dream side by side.

Your phantom wore the moon's cold mask,
   My phantom wore the same;
Forgetful of the feverish task
   In hope of which they came,
Each image held the other's eyes
And watched a grey distraction rise
   To cloud the eager flame –

To cloud the eager flame of love,
   To fog the shining gate;
They held the tyrannous queen above
   Sole mover of their fate,
They glared as marble statues glare
Across the tessellated stair
   Or down the halls of state.

And now warm earth was Arctic sea,
    Each breath came dagger-keen;
Two bergs of glinting ice were we,
    The broad moon sailed between;
There swam the mermaids, tailed and finned,
And love went by upon the wind
    As though it had not been.

Alice

When that prime heroine of our nation, Alice,
Climbing courageously in through the Palace
Of Looking Glass, found it inhabited
By chessboard personages, white and red,
Involved in never-ending tournament,
She being of a speculative bent
Had long foreshadowed something of the kind,
Asking herself: 'Suppose I stood behind
And viewed the fireplace of Their drawing-room
From hearthrug level, why must I assume
That what I'd see would need to correspond
With what I now see? And the rooms beyond?'
Proved right, yet not content with what she had done,
Alice decided to prolong her fun:
She set herself, with truly British pride
In being a pawn and playing for her side,
And simple faith in simple stratagem,
To learn the rules and moves and perfect them.
So prosperously there she settled down
That six moves only and she'd won her crown –
A triumph surely! But her greater feat
Was rounding these adventures off complete:
Accepting them, when safe returned again,
As queer but true – not only in the main

True, but as true as anything you'd swear to,
The usual three dimensions you are heir to.
For Alice though a child could understand
That neither did this chance-discovered land
Make nohow or contrariwise the clean
Dull round of mid-Victorian routine,
Nor did Victoria's golden rule extend
Beyond the glass: it came to the dead end
Where empty hearses turn about; thereafter
Begins that lubberland of dream and laughter,
The red-and-white-flower-spangled hedge, the grass
Where Apuleius pastured his Gold Ass,
Where young Gargantua made whole holiday. . .
But farther from our heroine not to stray,
Let us observe with what uncommon sense –
Though a secure and easy reference
Between Red Queen and Kitten could be found –
She made no false assumption on that ground
(A trap in which the scientist would fall)
That queens and kittens are identical.

Love Without Hope

Love without hope, as when the young bird-catcher
Swept off his tall hat to the Squire's own daughter,
So let the imprisoned larks escape and fly
Singing about her head, as she rode by.

Sergeant-Major Money

(1917)

It wasn't our battalion, but we lay alongside it,
  So the story is as true as the telling is frank.
They hadn't one Line-officer left, after Arras,
  Except a batty major and the Colonel, who drank.

'B' Company Commander was fresh from the Depôt,
  An expert on gas drill, otherwise a dud;
So Sergeant-Major Money carried on, as instructed,
  And that's where the swaddies began to sweat blood.

His Old Army humour was so well-spiced and hearty
  That one poor sod shot himself, and one lost his wits;
But discipline's maintained, and back in rest-billets
  The Colonel congratulates 'B' Company on their kits.

The subalterns went easy, as was only natural
  With a terror like Money driving the machine,
Till finally two Welshmen, butties from the Rhondda,
  Bayoneted their bugbear in a field-canteen.

Well, we couldn't blame the officers, they relied on Money;
  We couldn't blame the pitboys, their courage was grand;
Or, least of all, blame Money, an old stiff surviving
  In a New (bloody) Army he couldn't understand.

A Letter from Wales

(Richard Rolls to his friend, Captain Abel Wright)

This is a question of identity
Which I can't answer. Abel, I'll presume
On your good-nature, asking you to help me.
I hope you will, since you too are involved
As deeply in the problem as myself.
Who are we? Take down your old diary, please,
The one you kept in France, if you *are* you
Who served in the Black Fusiliers with me.
That is, again, of course, if I am I –
This isn't Descartes' philosophic doubt,
But, as I say, a question of identity,
And practical enough. – Turn up the date,
July the twenty-fourth, nineteen-sixteen,
And read the entry there:

                              'To-day I met
Meredith, transport-sergeant of the Second.
He told me that Dick Rolls had died of wounds.
I found out Doctor Dunn, and he confirms it;
Dunn says he wasn't in much pain, he thinks.'

Then the first draft of a verse-epitaph,
Expanded later into a moving poem.
'Death straddled on your bed: you groaned and tried
To stare him out, but in that death-stare died.'
Yes, died, poor fellow, the day he came of age.
But then appeared a second Richard Rolls
(Or that's the view that the facts force on me),
Showing Dick's features to support his claim
To rank and pay and friendship, Abel, with you.
And you acknowledged him as the old Dick,

Despite all evidence to the contrary,
Because, I think, you missed the dead too much.
You came up here to Wales to stay with him
And I don't know for sure, but I suspect
That you were dead too, killed at the Rectangle
One bloody morning of the same July,
The time that something snapped and sent you Berserk:
You ran across alone, with covering fire
Of a single rifle, routing the Saxons out
With bombs and yells and your wild eye; and stayed there
In careless occupation of the trench
For a full hour, reading, by all that's mad,
A book of pastoral poems! Then, they say,
Then you walked slowly back and went to sleep
Without reporting; that was the occasion,
No doubt, they killed you: it was your substitute
Strolled back and laid him down and woke as you,
Showing your features to support his claim
To rank and pay and friendship, Abel, with me.
So these two substitutes, yours and my own
(Though that's an Irish way of putting it,
For the I now talking is an honest I,
Independent of the I's now lost,
And a live dog's as good as a dead lion),
So, these two friends, the second of the series,
Came up to Wales pretending a wild joy
That they had cheated Death: they stayed together
At the same house and ate and drank and laughed
And wrote each other's poems, much too lazy
To write their own, and sat up every night
Talking and smoking almost until dawn.
Yes, they enjoyed life, but unless I now
Confound my present feeling, with the past,
They felt a sense of unreality

In the proceedings – stop! that's good, *proceedings*,
It suggests ghosts. – Well, then I want to ask you
Whether it really happened. Eating, laughing,
Sitting up late, writing each other's verses,
I might invent all that, but one thing happened
That seems too circumstantial for romance.
Can you confirm it? Yet, even if you can,
What does that prove? for who are you? or I?
Listen, it was a sunset. We were out
Climbing the mountain, eating blackberries;
Late afternoon, the third week in September,
The date's important: it might prove my point,
For unless Richard Rolls had really died
Could he have so recovered from his wounds
As to go climbing less than two months later?
And if it comes to that, what about you?
How had you come on sick-leave from the Line?
I don't remember you, that time, as wounded.
Anyhow . . . We were eating blackberries
By a wide field of tumbled boulderstones
Hedged with oaks and nut-trees. Gradually
A glamour spread about us, the low sun
Making the field unreal as a stage,
Gilding our faces with heroic light;
Then oaks and nut-boughs caught this golden flood,
Sending it back in a warm flare of green . . .
There was a mountain-ash among the boulders,
But too full-clustered and symmetrical
And highly coloured to convince as real.
We stopped blackberrying and someone said
(Was it I or you?) 'It is good for us to be here.'
The other said, 'Let us build Tabernacles'
(In honour of a new Transfiguration;
It was that sort of moment); but instead

I climbed up on the massive pulpit stone,
An old friend, but unreal with the rest,
And prophesied – not indeed of the future,
But declaimed poetry, and you climbed up too
And prophesied. The next thing I remember
Was a dragon scaly with fine-weather clouds
Poised high above the sun, and the sun dwindling
And then the second glory.
                                    You'll remember
That we were not then easily impressed
With pyrotechnics, whether God's or Man's.
We had seen the sun rise daily, weeks on end,
And watched the nightly rocket-shooting, varied
With red and green, and livened with gun-fire
And the loud single-bursting overgrown squib
Thrown from the minen-werfer: and one night
From a billet-window some ten miles away
We had watched the French making a mass-attack
At Notre Dame de Lorette, in a thunderstorm.
That was a grand display of all the Arts,
God's, Man's, the Devil's: in the course of which,
So lavishly the piece had been stage-managed,
A Frenchman was struck dead by a meteorite,
That was the sort of gala-show it was!
But this Welsh sunset, what shall I say of it?
It ended not at all as it began,
An influence rather than a spectacle
Raised to a strange degree beyond all wonder.
And I remember that we looked and found
A region of the sky below the dragon
Where we could gaze behind all time and space
And see as it were the colour of pure thought,
The texture of emptiness, and at that sight
We came away, not daring to see more:

Death was the price, we knew, of such perfection
And walking home . . .

                fell in with Captain Todd,
The Golf-Club Treasurer; he greeted us
With '*Did* you see that splendid sunset, boys?
Magnificent, was it not? I wonder now,
What writer could have done real justice to it
Except, of course, my old friend Walter Pater?
Ruskin perhaps? Yes, Ruskin might have done it.'

Well, *did* that happen, or am I just romancing?
And then again, one has to ask the question
What happened after to that *you* and *me*?
I have thought lately that they too got lost.
My representative went out once more
To France, and so did yours, and yours got killed,
Shot through the throat while bombing up a trench
At Bullecourt; if not there, then at least
On the thirteenth of July, nineteen eighteen,
Somewhere in the neighbourhood of Albert,
When you took a rifle bullet through the skull
Just after breakfast on a mad patrol.
But still you kept up the same stale pretence
As children do in nursery battle-games,
'No, I'm not dead. Look, I'm not even wounded.'
And I admit I followed your example,
Though nothing much happened that time in France.
I died at Hove after the Armistice,
Pneumonia, with the doctor's full consent.

I think the I and you who then took over
Rather forgot the part we used to play;
We wrote and saw each other often enough
And sent each other copies of new poems,

But there was a constraint in all our dealings,
A doubt, unformulated, but quite heavy
And not too well disguised. Something we guessed
Arising from the War, and yet the War
Was a forbidden ground of conversation.
Now *why*, can you say *why*, short of accepting
My substitution view? Then yesterday,
After five years of this relationship,
I found a relic of the second Richard,
A pack-valise marked with his name and rank . . .
And a sunset started, most unlike the other,
A pink-and-black depressing sort of show
Influenced by the Glasgow School of Art.
It sent me off on a long train of thought
And I began to feel badly confused,
Being accustomed to this newer self;
I wondered whether you could reassure me.
Now I have asked you, do you see my point?
What I'm asking really isn't 'Who am I?'
Or 'Who are you?' (you see my difficulty?)
But a stage before that, '*How am I to put*
The question that I'm asking you to answer?'

An Occasion

'The trenches are filled in, the houseless dead
Disperse and on the rising thunder-storm
Cast their weak limbs, are whirled up overhead
In clouds of fear. . .'
               Then suddenly as you read,
As we sat listening there, and cushioned warm,
War-scarred yet safe, alive beyond all doubt,
The blundering gale outside faltered, stood still:

Two bolts clicked at the glass doors, and a shrill
Impetuous gust of wind blew in with a shout,
Fluttering your poems. And the lamp went out.

Pure Death

We looked, we loved, and therewith instantly
Death became terrible to you and me.
By love we disenthralled our natural terror
From every comfortable philosopher
Or tall, grey doctor of divinity:
Death stood at last in his true rank and order.

It happened soon, so wild of heart were we,
Exchange of gifts grew to a malady:
Their worth rose always higher on each side
Till there seemed nothing but ungivable pride
That yet remained ungiven, and this degree
Called a conclusion not to be denied.

Then we at last bethought ourselves, made shift
And simultaneously this final gift
Gave: each with shaking hands unlocks
The sinister, long, brass-bound coffin-box,
Unwraps pure death, with such bewilderment
As greeted our love's first acknowledgement.

The Cool Web

Children are dumb to say how hot the day is,
How hot the scent is of the summer rose,
How dreadful the black wastes of evening sky,
How dreadful the tall soldiers drumming by.

But we have speech, to chill the angry day,
And speech, to dull the rose's cruel scent.
We spell away the overhanging night,
We spell away the soldiers and the fright.

There's a cool web of language winds us in,
Retreat from too much joy or too much fear:
We grow sea-green at last and coldly die
In brininess and volubility.

But if we let our tongues lose self-possession,
Throwing off language and its watery clasp
Before our death, instead of when death comes,
Facing the wide glare of the children's day,
Facing the rose, the dark sky and the drums,
We shall go mad no doubt and die that way.

Lost Acres

These acres, always again lost
    By every new ordnance-survey
And searched for at exhausting cost
    Of time and thought, are still away.

They have their paper-substitute –
    Intercalation of an inch
At the so-many-thousandth foot –
    And no one parish feels the pinch.

But lost they are, despite all care,
    And perhaps likely to be bound
Together in a piece somewhere,
    A plot of undiscovered ground.

Invisible, they have the spite
　　To swerve the tautest measuring-chain
And the exact theodolite
　　Perched every side of them in vain.

Yet, be assured, we have no need
　　To plot these acres of the mind
With prehistoric fern and reed
　　And monsters such as heroes find.

Maybe they have their flowers, their birds,
　　Their trees behind the phantom fence,
But of a substance without words:
　　To walk there would be loss of sense.

Sick Love

O Love, be fed with apples while you may,
And feel the sun and go in royal array,
A smiling innocent on the heavenly causeway,

Though in what listening horror for the cry
That soars in outer blackness dismally,
The dumb blind beast, the paranoiac fury:

Be warm, enjoy the season, lift your head,
Exquisite in the pulse of tainted blood,
That shivering glory not to be despised.

Take your delight in momentariness,
Walk between dark and dark – a shining space
With the grave's narrowness, though not its peace.

In Broken Images

He is quick, thinking in clear images;
I am slow, thinking in broken images.

He becomes dull, trusting to his clear images;
I become sharp, mistrusting my broken images.

Trusting his images, he assumes their relevance;
Mistrusting my images, I question their relevance.

Assuming their relevance, he assumes the fact;
Questioning their relevance, I question the fact.

When the fact fails him, he questions his senses;
When the fact fails me, I approve my senses.

He continues quick and dull in his clear images;
I continue slow and sharp in my broken images.

He in a new confusion of his understanding;
I in a new understanding of my confusion.

Warning to Children

Children, if you dare to think
Of the greatness, rareness, muchness,
Fewness of this precious only
Endless world in which you say
You live, you think of things like this:
Blocks of slate enclosing dappled
Red and green, enclosing tawny
Yellow nets, enclosing white
And black acres of dominoes,
Where a neat brown paper parcel
Tempts you to untie the string.

In the parcel a small island,
On the island a large tree,
On the tree a husky fruit.
Strip the husk and pare the rind off:
In the kernel you will see
Blocks of slate enclosed by dappled
Red and green, enclosed by tawny
Yellow nets, enclosed by white
And black acres of dominoes,
Where the same brown paper parcel –
Children, leave the string alone!
For who dares undo the parcel
Finds himself at once inside it,
On the island, in the fruit,
Blocks of slate about his head,
Finds himself enclosed by dappled
Green and red, enclosed by yellow
Tawny nets, enclosed by black
And white acres of dominoes,
With the same brown paper parcel
Still unopened on his knee.
And, if he then should dare to think
Of the fewness, muchness, rareness,
Greatness of this endless only
Precious world in which he says
He lives – he then unties the string.

Welsh Incident

'But that was nothing to what things came out
From the sea-caves of Criccieth yonder.'
'What were they? Mermaids? dragons? ghosts?'

'Nothing at all of any things like that.'
'What were they, then?'
                            'All sorts of queer things,
Things never seen or heard or written about,
Very strange, un-Welsh, utterly peculiar
Things. Oh, solid enough they seemed to touch,
Had anyone dared it. Marvellous creation,
All various shapes and sizes, and no sizes,
All new, each perfectly unlike his neighbour,
Though all came moving slowly out together.'
'Describe just one of them.'
                            'I am unable.'
'What were their colours?'
                            'Mostly nameless colours,
Colours you'd like to see; but one was puce
Or perhaps more like crimson, but not purplish.
Some had no colour.'
                            'Tell me, had they legs?'
'Not a leg nor foot among them that I saw.'
'But did these things come out in any order?
What o'clock was it? What was the day of the week?
Who else was present? How was the weather?'
'I was coming to that. It was half-past three
On Easter Tuesday last. The sun was shining.
The Harlech Silver Band played *Marchog Jesu*
On thirty-seven shimmering instruments,
Collecting for Caernarvon's (Fever) Hospital Fund.
The populations of Pwllheli, Criccieth,
Portmadoc, Borth, Tremadoc, Penrhyndeudraeth,
Were all assembled. Criccieth's mayor addressed them
First in good Welsh and then in fluent English,
Twisting his fingers in his chain of office,
Welcoming the things. They came out on the sand,

Not keeping time to the band, moving seaward
Silently at a snail's pace. But at last
The most odd, indescribable thing of all,
Which hardly one man there could see for wonder,
Did something recognizably a something.'
'Well, what?'

                  'It made a noise.'

                                 'A frightening noise?'
'No, no.'

                 'A musical noise? A noise of scuffling?'
'No, but a very loud, respectable noise –
Like groaning to oneself on Sunday morning
In Chapel, close before the second psalm.'
'What did the mayor do?'

                                'I was coming to that.'

Nature's Lineaments

When mountain rocks and leafy trees
And clouds and things like these,
With edges,

Caricature the human face,
Such scribblings have no grace
Nor peace –

The bulbous nose, the sunken chin,
The ragged mouth in grin
Of cretin.

Nature is always so: you find
That all she has of mind
Is wind,

Retching among the empty spaces,
Ruffling the idiot grasses,
The sheep's fleeces.

Whose pleasures are excreting, poking,
Havocking and sucking,
Sleepy licking.

Whose griefs are melancholy,
Whose flowers are oafish,
Whose waters, silly,
Whose birds, raffish,
Whose fish, fish.

Wm. Brazier

At the end of Tarriers' Lane, which was the street
We children thought the pleasantest in Town
Because of the old elms growing from the pavement
And the crookedness, when the other streets were straight,
[They were always at the lamp-post round the corner,
Those pugs and papillons and in-betweens,
Nosing and snuffling for the latest news]
Lived Wm. Brazier, with a gilded sign,
'Practical Chimney Sweep'. He had black hands,
Black face, black clothes, black brushes and white teeth;
He jingled round the town in a pony-trap,
And the pony's name was Soot, and Soot was black.
But the brass fittings on the trap, the shafts,
On Soot's black harness, on the black whip-butt,
Twinkled and shone like any guardsman's buttons.
Wasn't that pretty? And when we children jeered:
'Hello, Wm. Brazier! Dirty-face Wm. Brazier!'

He would crack his whip at us and smile and bellow,
'Hello, my dears!' [If he were drunk, but otherwise:
'Scum off, you damned young milliners' bastards, you!']

Let them copy it out on a pink page of their albums,
Carefully leaving out the bracketed lines.
It's an old story – f's for s's –
But good enough for them, the suckers.

A Former Attachment

And glad to find, on again looking at it,
It meant even less to me than I had thought –
You know the ship is moving when you see
The boxes on the quayside slide away
And become smaller – and feel a calm delight
When the port's cleared and the coast out of sight,
And ships are few, each on its proper course,
With no occasion for approach or discourse.

Return Fare

And so to Ireland on an Easter Tuesday
To a particular place I could not find.
A sleeping man beside me in the boat-train
Sat whistling Liliburlero in his sleep;
Not, I had thought, a possible thing, yet so.
And through a port-hole of the Fishguard boat,
That was the hospital-boat of twelve years back,
Passengered as before with doubt and dying,
I saw the moon through glass, but a waning moon –
Bad luck, self-doubtful, so once more I slept.

And then the engines woke me up by stopping.
The piers of the quay loomed up. So I went up.
The sun shone rainily and jokingly,
And everyone joked at his own expense,
And the priest declared 'nothing but fishing tackle,'
Laughing provokingly. I could not laugh.
And the hard cackling laughter of the men
And the false whinnying laughter of the girls
Grieved me. The telegraph-clerk said, grieving too,
'St Peter, he's two words in the Free State now,
So that's a salmon due.' I paid the fish.
And everyone I asked about the place
Knew the place well, but not its whereabouts,
And the black-shawled peasant woman asked me then,
Wasn't I jaded? And she grieved to me
Of the apple and the expulsion from the garden.
Ireland went by, and went by as I saw her
When last I saw her for the first time
Exactly how I had seen her all the time.
And I found the place near Sligo, not the place,
So back to England on the Easter Thursday.

It Was All Very Tidy

When I reached his place,
The grass was smooth,
The wind was delicate,
The wit well timed,
The limbs well formed,
The pictures straight on the wall:
It was all very tidy.

He was cancelling out
The last row of figures,
He had his beard tied up in ribbons,
There was no dust on his shoe,
Everyone nodded:
It was all very tidy.

Music was not playing,
There were no sudden noises,
The sun shone blandly,
The clock ticked:
It was all very tidy.

'Apart from and above all this,'
I reassured myself,
'There is now myself.'
It was all very tidy.

Death did not address me,
He had nearly done:
It was all very tidy.

They asked, did I not think
It was all very tidy?

I could not bring myself
To laugh, or untie
His beard's neat ribbons,
Or jog his elbow,
Or whistle, or sing,
Or make disturbance.
I consented, frozenly,
He was unexceptionable:
It was all very tidy.

The Reader Over My Shoulder

You, reading over my shoulder, peering beneath
My writing arm – I suddenly feel your breath
   Hot on my hand or on my nape,
So interrupt my theme, scratching these few
Words on the margin for you, namely you,
   Too-human shape fixed in that shape: –

All the saying of things against myself
And for myself I have well done myself.
   What now, old enemy, shall you do
But quote and underline, thrusting yourself
Against me, as ambassador of myself,
   In damned confusion of myself and you?

For you in strutting, you in sycophancy,
Have played too long this other self of me,
   Doubling the part of judge and patron
With that of creaking grind-stone to my wit.
Know me, have done: I am a proud spirit
   And you for ever clay. Have done!

New Legends

Content in you,
Andromeda serene,
Mistress of air and ocean
And every fiery dragon,
Chained to no cliff,
Asking no rescue of me.

Content in you,
Mad Atalanta,
Stooping unpausing,
Ever ahead,
Acquitting me of rivalry.

Content in you
Who made King Proteus marvel,
Showing him singleness
Past all variety.

Content in you,
Niobe of no children,
Of no calamity.

Content in you,
Helen, foiler of beauty.

The Terraced Valley

In a deep thought of you and concentration
I came by hazard to a new region:
The unnecessary sun was not there,
The necessary earth lay without care –
For more than sunshine warmed the skin
Of the round world that was turned outside-in.

Calm sea beyond the terraced valley
Without horizon easily was spread,
As it were overhead,
Washing the mountain spurs behind me:
The unnecessary sky was not there,
Therefore no heights, no deeps, no birds of the air.

Neat outside-inside, neat below-above,
Hermaphrodizing love.
Neat this-way-that-way and without mistake:
On the right hand could slide the left glove.
Neat over-under: the young snake
Through an unyielding shell his path could break.
Singing of kettles, like a singing brook,
Made out-of-doors a fireside nook.

But you, my love, where had you then your station?
Seeing that on this counter-earth together
We go not distant from each other;
I knew you near me in that strange region,
So searched for you, in hope to see you stand
On some near olive-terrace, in the heat,
The left-hand glove drawn on your right hand,
The empty snake's egg perfect at your feet –

But found you nowhere in the wide land,
And cried disconsolately, until you spoke
Immediate at my elbow, and your voice broke
This trick of time, changing the world about
To once more inside-in and outside-out.

Flying Crooked

The butterfly, a cabbage-white,
(His honest idiocy of flight)
Will never now, it is too late,
Master the art of flying straight,
Yet has – who knows so well as I? –
A just sense of how not to fly:

He lurches here and here by guess
And God and hope and hopelessness.
Even the aerobatic swift
Has not his flying-crooked gift.

Time

The vague sea thuds against the marble cliffs
And from their fragments age-long grinds
Pebbles like flowers.

Or the vague weather wanders in the fields,
And up spring flowers with coloured buds
Like marble pebbles.

The beauty of the flowers is Time, death-grieved;
The pebbles' beauty too is Time,
Life-wearied.

It is easy to admire a blowing flower
Or a smooth pebble flower-like freaked
By Time and vagueness.

Time is Time's lapse, the emulsive element coaxing
All obstinate locks and rusty hinges
To loving-kindness.

And am I proof against that lovesome pair,
Old age and childhood, twins in Time,
In sorrowful vagueness?

And will I not pretend the accustomed thanks:
Humouring age with filial flowers,
Childhood with pebbles?

[48]

The Legs

There was this road,
And it led up-hill,
And it led down-hill,
And round and in and out.

And the traffic was legs,
Legs from the knees down,
Coming and going,
Never pausing.

And the gutters gurgled
With the rain's overflow,
And the sticks on the pavement
Blindly tapped and tapped.

What drew the legs along
Was the never-stopping,
And the senseless, frightening
Fate of being legs.

Legs for the road,
The road for legs,
Resolutely nowhere
In both directions.

My legs at least
Were not in that rout:
On grass by the roadside
Entire I stood,

Watching the unstoppable
Legs go by
With never a stumble
Between step and step.

Though my smile was broad
The legs could not see,
Though my laugh was loud
The legs could not hear.

My head dizzied, then:
I wondered suddenly,
Might I too be a walker
From the knees down?

Gently I touched my shins.
The doubt unchained them:
They had run in twenty puddles
Before I regained them.

Ogres and Pygmies

Those famous men of old, the Ogres –
They had long beards and stinking arm-pits,
They were wide-mouthed, long-yarded and great-bellied
Yet not of taller stature, Sirs, than you.
They lived on Ogre-Strand, which was no place
But the churl's terror of their vast extent,
Where every foot was three-and-thirty inches
And every penny bought a whole hog.
Now of their company none survive, not one,
The times being, thank God, unfavourable
To all but nightmare shadows of their fame;
Their images stand howling on the hill
(The winds enforced against those wide mouths),
Whose granite haunches country-folk salute
With May Day kisses, and whose knobbed knees.

So many feats they did to admiration:
With their enormous throats they sang louder
Than ten cathedral choirs, with their grand yards
Stormed the most rare and obstinate maidenheads,
With their strong-gutted and capacious bellies
Digested stones and glass like ostriches.
They dug great pits and heaped huge mounds,
Deflected rivers, wrestled with the bear
And hammered judgements for posterity –
For the sweet-cupid-lipped and tassel-yarded
Delicate-stomached dwellers
In Pygmy Alley, where with brooding on them
A foot is shrunk to seven inches
And twelve-pence will not buy a spare rib.
And who would judge between Ogres and Pygmies –
The thundering text, the snivelling commentary –
Reading between such covers he will marvel
How his own members bloat and shrink again.

On Portents

If strange things happen where she is,
So that men say that graves open
And the dead walk, or that futurity
Becomes a womb and the unborn are shed,
Such portents are not to be wondered at,
Being tourbillions in Time made
By the strong pulling of her bladed mind
Through that ever-reluctant element.

The Bards

The bards falter in shame, their running verse
Stumbles, with marrow-bones the drunken diners
Pelt them for their delay.
It is a something fearful in the song
Plagues them – an unknown grief that like a churl
Goes commonplace in cowskin
And bursts unheralded, crowing and coughing,
An unpilled holly-club twirled in his hand,
Into their many-shielded, samite-curtained,
Jewel-bright hall where twelve kings sit at chess
Over the white-bronze pieces and the gold;
And by a gross enchantment
Flails down the rafters and leads off the queens –
The wild-swan-breasted, the rose-ruddy-cheeked
Raven-haired daughters of their admiration –
To stir his black pots and to bed on straw.

Ulysses

To the much-tossed Ulysses, never done
    With woman whether gowned as wife or whore,
Penelope and Circe seemed as one:
She like a whore made his lewd fancies run,
    And wifely she a hero to him bore.

Their counter-changings terrified his way:
    They were the clashing rocks, Symplegades,
Scylla and Charybdis too were they;
Now angry storms frosting the sea with spray
    And now the lotus island's drunken ease.

They multiplied into the Sirens' throng,
  Forewarned by fear of whom he stood bound fast
Hand and foot helpless to the vessel's mast,
Yet would not stop his ears: daring their song
  He groaned and sweated till that shore was past.

One, two and many: flesh had made him blind,
  Flesh had one pleasure only in the act,
Flesh set one purpose only in the mind –
Triumph of flesh and afterwards to find
  Still those same terrors wherewith flesh was racked.

His wiles were witty and his fame far known,
Every king's daughter sought him for her own,
  Yet he was nothing to be won or lost,
  All lands to him were Ithaca: love-tossed
He loathed the fraud, yet would not bed alone.

Down, Wanton, Down!

Down, wanton, down! Have you no shame
That at the whisper of Love's name,
  Or Beauty's, presto! up you raise
  Your angry head and stand at gaze?

Poor bombard-captain, sworn to reach
The ravelin and effect a breach –
Indifferent what you storm or why,
So be that in the breach you die!

Love may be blind, but Love at least
Knows what is man and what mere beast;
Or Beauty wayward, but requires
More delicacy from her squires.

Tell me, my witless, whose one boast
Could be your staunchness at the post,
When were you made a man of parts
To think fine and profess the arts?

Will many-gifted Beauty come
Bowing to your bald rule of thumb,
Or Love swear loyalty to your crown?
Be gone, have done! Down, wanton, down!

Nobody

Nobody, ancient mischief, nobody,
Harasses always with an absent body.

Nobody coming up the road, nobody,
Like a tall man in a dark cloak, nobody.

Nobody about the house, nobody,
Like children creeping up the stairs, nobody.

Nobody anywhere in the garden, nobody,
Like a young girl quiet with needlework, nobody.

Nobody coming, nobody, not yet here,
Incessantly welcomed by the wakeful ear.

Until this nobody shall consent to die
Under his curse must everyone lie –

The curse of his envy, of his grief and fright,
Of sudden rape and murder screamed in the night.

The Christmas Robin

The snows of February had buried Christmas
Deep in the woods, where grew self-seeded
The fir-trees of a Christmas yet unknown,
Without a candle or a strand of tinsel.

Nevertheless when, hand in hand, plodding
Between the frozen ruts, we lovers paused
And 'Christmas trees!' cried suddenly together,
Christmas was there again, as in December.

We velveted our love with fantasy
Down a long vista-row of Christmas trees,
Whose coloured candles slowly guttered down
As grandchildren came trooping round our knees.

But he knew better, did the Christmas robin –
The murderous robin with his breast aglow
And legs apart, in a spade-handle perched:
He prophesied more snow, and worse than snow.

At First Sight

'Love at first sight,' some say, misnaming
Discovery of twinned helplessness
Against the huge tug of procreation.

But friendship at first sight? This also
Catches fiercely at the surprised heart
So that the cheek blanches and then blushes.

Recalling War

Entrance and exit wounds are silvered clean,
The track aches only when the rain reminds.
The one-legged man forgets his leg of wood,
The one-armed man his jointed wooden arm.
The blinded man sees with his ears and hands
As much or more than once with both his eyes.
Their war was fought these twenty years ago
And now assumes the nature-look of time,
As when the morning traveller turns and views
His wild night-stumbling carved into a hill.

What, then, was war? No mere discord of flags
But an infection of the common sky
That sagged ominously upon the earth
Even when the season was the airiest May.
Down pressed the sky, and we, oppressed, thrust
    out
Boastful tongue, clenched fist and valiant yard.
Natural infirmities were out of mode,
For Death was young again: patron alone
Of healthy dying, premature fate-spasm.

Fear made fine bed-fellows. Sick with delight
At life's discovered transitoriness,
Our youth became all-flesh and waived the mind.
Never was such antiqueness of romance,
Such tasty honey oozing from the heart.
And old importances came swimming back –
Wine, meat, log-fires, a roof over the head,
A weapon at the thigh, surgeons at call.
Even there was a use again for God –
A word of rage in lack of meat, wine, fire,
In ache of wounds beyond all surgeoning.

War was return of earth to ugly earth,
War was foundering of sublimities,
Extinction of each happy art and faith
By which the world had still kept head in air,
Protesting logic or protesting love,
Until the unendurable moment struck –
The inward scream, the duty to run mad.

And we recall the merry ways of guns –
Nibbling the walls of factory and church
Like a child, piecrust; felling groves of trees
Like a child, dandelions with a switch.
Machine-guns rattle toy-like from a hill,
Down in a row the brave tin-soldiers fall:
A sight to be recalled in elder days
When learnedly the future we devote
To yet more boastful visions of despair.

To Walk On Hills

To walk on hills is to employ legs
As porters of the head and heart
Jointly adventuring towards
Perhaps true equanimity.

To walk on hills is to see sights
And hear sounds unfamiliar.
When in wind the pine-tree roars,
When crags with bleatings echo,
When water foams below the fall,
Heart records that journey
As memorable indeed;
Head reserves opinion,
Confused by the wind.

A view of three shires and the sea!
Seldom so much at once appears
Of the coloured world, says heart.
Head is glum, says nothing.

Legs become weary, halting
To sprawl in a rock's shelter,
While the sun drowsily blinks
On head at last brought low –
This giddied passenger of legs
That has no word to utter.

Heart does double duty,
As heart, and as head,
With portentous trifling.
A castle, on its crag perched,
Across the miles between is viewed
With awe as across years.

Now a daisy pleases,
Pleases and astounds, even,
That on a garden lawn could blow
All summer long with no esteem.

And the buzzard's cruel poise,
And the plover's misery,
And the important beetle's
Blue-green-shiny back. . .

To walk on hills is to employ legs
To march away and lose the day.
Tell us, have you known shepherds?
And are they not a witless race,
Prone to quaint visions?
Not thus from solitude
(Solitude sobers only)
But from long hilltop striding.

To Bring the Dead to Life

To bring the dead to life
Is no great magic.
Few are wholly dead:
Blow on a dead man's embers
And a live flame will start.

Let his forgotten griefs be now,
And now his withered hopes;
Subdue your pen to his handwriting
Until it prove as natural
To sign his name as yours.

Limp as he limped,
Swear by the oaths he swore;
If he wore black, affect the same;
If he had gouty fingers,
Be yours gouty too.

Assemble tokens intimate of him –
A seal, a cloak, a pen:
Around these elements then build
A home familiar to
The greedy revenant.

So grant him life, but reckon
That the grave which housed him
May not be empty now:
You in his spotted garments
Shall yourself lie wrapped.

To Evoke Posterity

To evoke posterity
Is to weep on your own grave,
Ventriloquizing for the unborn:
'Would you were present in flesh, hero!
What wreaths and junketings!'

And the punishment is fixed:
To be found fully ancestral,
To be cast in bronze for a city square,
To dribble green in times of rain
And stain the pedestal.

Spiders in the spread beard;
A life proverbial
On clergy lips a-cackle;
Eponymous institutes,
Their luckless architecture.

Two more dates of life and birth
For the hour of special study
From which all boys and girls of mettle
Twice a week play truant
And worn excuses try.

Alive, you have abhorred
The crowds on holiday
Jostling and whistling – yet would you air
Your death-mask, smoothly lidded
Along the promenade?

Any Honest Housewife

Any honest housewife could sort them out,
Having a nose for fish, an eye for apples.
Is it any mystery who are the sound,
And who the rotten? Never, by her lights.

Any honest housewife who, by ill-fortune,
Ever engaged a slut to scrub for her
Could instantly distinguish from the workers
The lazy, the liars, and the petty thieves.

Does this denote a sixth peculiar sense
Gifted to housewives for their vestal needs?
Or is it failure of the usual five
In all unthrifty writers on this head?

Never Such Love

Twined together and, as is customary,
For words of rapture groping, they
'Never such love,' swore, 'ever before was!'
Contrast with all loves that had failed or staled
Registered their own as love indeed.

And was this not to blab idly
The heart's fated inconstancy?
Better in love to seal the love-sure lips,
For truly love was before words were,
And no word given, no word broken.

When the name 'love' is uttered
(Love, the near-honourable malady
With which in greed and haste they
Each other do infect and curse)
Or, worse, is written down. . .

Wise after the event, by love withered,
A 'never more!' most frantically
Sorrow and shame would proclaim
Such as, they'd swear, never before were:
True lovers even in this.

Like Snow

She, then, like snow in a dark night,
Fell secretly. And the world waked
With dazzling of the drowsy eye,
So that some muttered 'Too much light',
And drew the curtains close.
Like snow, warmer than fingers feared,
And to soil friendly;
Holding the histories of the night
In yet unmelted tracks.

The Climate of Thought

The climate of thought has seldom been described.
It is no terror of Caucasian frost,
Nor yet that brooding Hindu heat
For which a loin-rag and a dish of rice
Suffice until the pestilent monsoon.
But, without winter, blood would run too thin;
Or, without summer, fires would burn too long.
In thought the seasons run concurrently.

Thought has a sea to gaze, not voyage, on;
And hills, to rough the edge of the bland sky,
Not to be climbed in search of blander prospect;

Few birds, sufficient for such caterpillars
As are not fated to turn butterflies;
Few butterflies, sufficient for such flowers
As are the luxury of a full orchard;
Wind, sometimes, in the evening chimneys; rain
On the early morning roof, on sleepy sight;
Snow streaked upon the hilltop, feeding
The fond brook at the valley-head
That greens the valley and that parts the lips;
The sun, simple, like a country neighbour;
The moon, grand, not fanciful with clouds.

End of Play

We have reached the end of pastime, for always,
Ourselves and everyone, though few confess it
Or see the sky other than, as of old,
A foolish smiling Mary-mantle blue;

Though life may still seem to dawdle golden
In some June landscape among giant flowers,
The grass to shine as cruelly green as ever,
Faith to descend in a chariot from the sky –

May seem only: a mirror and an echo
Mediate henceforth with vision and sound.
The cry of faith, no longer mettlesome,
Sounds as a blind man's pitiful plea of 'blind'.

We have at last ceased idling, which to regret
Were as shallow as to ask our milk-teeth back;
As many forthwith do, and on their knees
Call lugubriously upon chaste Christ.

We tell no lies now, at last cannot be
The rogues we were – so evilly linked in sense
With what we scrutinized that lion or tiger
Could leap from every copse, strike and devour us.

No more shall love in hypocritic pomp
Conduct its innocents through a dance of shame,
From timid touching of gloved fingers
To frantic laceration of naked breasts.

Yet love survives, the word carved on a sill
Under antique dread of the headsman's axe;
It is the echoing mind, as in the mirror
We stare on our dazed trunks at the block kneeling.

Leaving the Rest Unsaid

Finis, apparent on an earlier page,
With fallen obelisk for colophon,
Must this be here repeated?

Death has been ruefully announced
And to die once is death enough,
Be sure, for any life-time.

Must the book end, as you would end it,
With testamentary appendices
And graveyard indices?

But no, I will not lay me down
To let your tearful music mar
The decent mystery of my progress.

So now, my solemn ones, leaving the rest unsaid,
Rising in air as on a gander's wing
At a careless comma,

[64]

The Thieves

Lovers in the act dispense
With such meum-tuum sense
As might warningly reveal
What they must not pick or steal,
And their nostrum is to say:
'I and you are both away.'

After, when they disentwine
You from me and yours from mine,
Neither can be certain who
Was that I whose mine was you.
To the act again they go
More completely not to know.

Theft is theft and raid is raid
Though reciprocally made.
Lovers, the conclusion is
Doubled sighs and jealousies
In a single heart that grieves
For lost honour among thieves.

Dawn Bombardment

Guns from the sea open against us:
The smoke rocks bodily in the casemate
And a yell of doom goes up.
We count and bless each new, heavy concussion –
Captives awaiting rescue.

Visiting angel of the wild-fire hair
Who in dream reassured us nightly
Where we lay fettered,
Laugh at us, as we wake – our faces
So tense with hope the tears run down.

Lollocks

By sloth on sorrow fathered,
These dusty-featured Lollocks
Have their nativity in all disordered
Backs of cupboard drawers.

They play hide and seek
Among collars and novels
And empty medicine bottles,
And letters from abroad
That never will be answered.

Every sultry night
They plague little children,
Gurgling from the cistern,
Humming from the air,
Skewing up the bed-clothes,
Twitching the blind.

When the imbecile agèd
Are over-long in dying
And the nurse drowses,
Lollocks come skipping
Up the tattered stairs
And are nasty together
In the bed's shadow.

The signs of their presence
Are boils on the neck,
Dreams of vexation suddenly recalled
In the middle of the morning,
Languor after food.

Men cannot see them,
Men cannot hear them,

Do not believe in them –
But suffer the more
Both in neck and belly.

Women can see them –
O those naughty wives
Who sit by the fireside
Munching bread and honey,
Watching them in mischief
From corners of their eyes,
Slily allowing them to lick
Honey-sticky fingers.

Sovereign against Lollocks
Are hard broom and soft broom,
To well comb the hair,
To well brush the shoe,
And to pay every debt
As it falls due.

Despite and Still

Have you not read
The words in my head,
And I made part
Of your own heart?
We have been such as draw
The losing straw –
You of your gentleness,
I of my rashness,
Both of despair –
Yet still might share
This happy will:
To love despite and still.

Never let us deny
The thing's necessity,
But, O, refuse
To choose
Where chance may seem to give
Loves in alternative.

The Suicide in the Copse

The suicide, far from content,
Stared down at his own shattered skull:
Was this what he meant?

Had not his purpose been
To liberate himself from duns and dolts
By a change of scene?

From somewhere came a roll of laughter:
He had looked so on his wedding-day,
And the day after.

There was nowhere at all to go,
And no diversion now but to peruse
What literature the winds might blow

Into the copse where his body lay:
A year-old sheet of sporting news,
A crumpled schoolboy essay.

Mid-Winter Waking

Stirring suddenly from long hibernation,
I knew myself once more a poet
Guarded by timeless principalities
Against the worm of death, this hillside haunting;
And presently dared open both my eyes.

O gracious, lofty, shone against from under,
Back-of-the-mind-far clouds like towers;
And you, sudden warm airs that blow
Before the expected season of new blossom,
While sheep still gnaw at roots and lambless go –

Be witness that on waking, this mid-winter,
I found her hand in mine laid closely
Who shall watch out the Spring with me.
We stared in silence all around us
But found no winter anywhere to see.

The Beach

Louder than gulls the little children scream
Whom fathers haul into the jovial foam;
But others fearlessly rush in, breast high,
Laughing the salty water from their mouths –
Heroes of the nursery.

The horny boatman, who has seen whales
And flying fishes, who has sailed as far
As Demerara and the Ivory Coast,
Will warn them, when they crowd to hear his tales,
That every ocean smells alike of tar.

The Door

When she came suddenly in
It seemed the door could never close again,
Nor even did she close it – she, she –
The room lay open to a visiting sea
Which no door could restrain.

Yet when at last she smiled, tilting her head
To take her leave of me,
Where she had smiled, instead
There was a dark door closing endlessly,
The waves receded.

Under the Pot

Sulkily the sticks burn, and though they crackle
  With scorn under the bubbling pot, or spout
Magnanimous jets of flame against the smoke,
  At each heel end a dirty sap breaks out.

Confess, creatures, how sulkily ourselves
  We hiss with doom, fuel of a sodden age –
Not rapt up roaring to the chimney stack
  On incandescent clouds of spirit or rage.

Through Nightmare

Never be disenchanted of
That place you sometimes dream yourself into,
Lying at large remove beyond all dream,
Or those you find there, though but seldom
In their company seated –

The untameable, the live, the gentle.
Have you not known them? Whom? They carry
Time looped so river-wise about their house
There's no way in by history's road
To name or number them.

In your sleepy eyes I read the journey
Of which disjointedly you tell; which stirs
My loving admiration, that you should travel
Through nightmare to a lost and moated land,
Who are timorous by nature.

To Lucia at Birth

Though the moon beaming matronly and bland
  Greets you, among the crowd of the new-born,
With 'welcome to the world' yet understand
  That still her pale, lascivious unicorn
And bloody lion are loose on either hand:
  With din of bones and tantarará of horn
Their fanciful cortège parades the land –
  Pest on the highroad, wild-fire in the corn.

Outrageous company to be born into,
  Lunatics of a royal age long dead.
Then reckon time by what you are or do,
  Not by the epochs of the war they spread.
  Hark how they roar; but never turn your head.
Nothing will change them, let them not change you.

She Tells Her Love While Half Asleep

She tells her love while half asleep,
   In the dark hours,
      With half-words whispered low:
As Earth stirs in her winter sleep
   And puts out grass and flowers
      Despite the snow,
      Despite the falling snow.

Instructions to the Orphic Adept

[In part translated from the Timpone Grande *and*
Campagno Orphic *tablets.]*

So soon as ever your mazed spirit descends
From daylight into darkness, Man, remember
What you have suffered here in Samothrace,
What you have suffered.

After your passage through Hell's seven floods,
Whose fumes of sulphur will have parched your throat,
The Halls of Judgement shall loom up before you,
A miracle of jasper and of onyx.
To the left hand there bubbles a black spring
Overshadowed with a great white cypress.
Avoid this spring, which is Forgetfulness;
Though all the common rout rush down to drink,
Avoid this spring!

To the right hand there lies a secret pool
Alive with speckled trout and fish of gold;
A hazel overshadows it. Ophion,
Primaeval serpent straggling in the branches,

Darts out his tongue. This holy pool is fed
By dripping water; guardians stand before it.
Run to this pool, the pool of Memory,
Run to this pool!

Then will the guardians scrutinize you, saying:
'Who are you, who? What have you to remember?
Do you not fear Ophion's flickering tongue?
Go rather to the spring beneath the cypress,
Flee from this pool!'

Then you shall answer: 'I am parched with thirst.
Give me to drink. I am a child of Earth,
But of Sky also, come from Samothrace.
Witness the glint of amber on my brow.
Out of the Pure I come, as you may see.
I also am of your thrice-blessèd kin,
Child of the three-fold Queen of Samothrace;
Have made full quittance for my deeds of blood,
Have been by her invested in sea-purple,
And like a kid have fallen into milk.
Give me to drink, now I am parched with thirst,
Give me to drink!'

But they will ask you yet: 'What of your feet?'
You shall reply: 'My feet have borne me here
Out of the weary wheel, the circling years,
To that still, spokeless wheel: – Persephone.
Give me to drink!'

Then they will welcome you with fruit and flowers,
And lead you toward the ancient dripping hazel,
Crying: 'Brother of our immortal blood,
Drink and remember glorious Samothrace!'
Then you shall drink.

You shall drink deep of that refreshing draught,
To become lords of the uninitiated
Twittering ghosts, Hell's countless populace –
To become heroes, knights upon swift horses,
Pronouncing oracles from tall white tombs
By the nymphs tended. They with honey water
Shall pour libations to your serpent shapes,
That you may drink.

Theseus and Ariadne

High on his figured couch beyond the waves
He dreams, in dream recalling her set walk
Down paths of oyster-shell bordered with flowers,
Across the shadowy turf below the vines.
He sighs: 'Deep sunk in my erroneous past
She haunts the ruins and the ravaged lawns.'

Yet still unharmed it stands, the regal house
Crooked with age and overtopped by pines
Where first he wearied of her constancy.
And with a surer foot she goes than when
Dread of his hate was thunder in the air,
When the pines agonized with flaws of wind
And flowers glared up at her with frantic eyes.
Of him, now all is done, she never dreams
But calls a living blessing down upon
What he supposes rubble and rank grass;
Playing the queen to nobler company.

To Juan at the Winter Solstice

There is one story and one story only
That will prove worth your telling,
Whether as learned bard or gifted child;
To it all lines or lesser gauds belong
That startle with their shining
Such common stories as they stray into.

Is it of trees you tell, their months and virtues,
Or strange beasts that beset you,
Of birds that croak at you the Triple will?
Or of the Zodiac and how slow it turns
Below the Boreal Crown,
Prison of all true kings that ever reigned?

Water to water, ark again to ark,
From woman back to woman:
So each new victim treads unfalteringly
The never altered circuit of his fate,
Bringing twelve peers as witness
Both to his starry rise and starry fall.

Or is it of the Virgin's silver beauty,
All fish below the thighs?
She in her left hand bears a leafy quince;
When with her right she crooks a finger, smiling,
How may the King hold back?
Royally then he barters life for love.

Or of the undying snake from chaos hatched,
Whose coils contain the ocean,
Into whose chops with naked sword he springs,
Then in black water, tangled by the reeds,
Battles three days and nights,
To be spewed up beside her scalloped shore?

Much snow is falling, winds roar hollowly,
The owl hoots from the elder,
Fear in your heart cries to the loving-cup:
Sorrow to sorrow as the sparks fly upward.
The log groans and confesses:
There is one story and one story only.

Dwell on her graciousness, dwell on her smiling,
Do not forget what flowers
The great boar trampled down in ivy time.
Her brow was creamy as the crested wave,
Her sea-grey eyes were wild
But nothing promised that is not performed.

The Persian Version

Truth-loving Persians do not dwell upon
The trivial skirmish fought near Marathon.
As for the Greek theatrical tradition
Which represents that summer's expedition
Not as a mere reconnaissance in force
By three brigades of foot and one of horse
(Their left flank covered by some obsolete
Light craft detached from the main Persian fleet)
But as a grandiose, ill-starred attempt
To conquer Greece – they treat it with contempt;
And only incidentally refute
Major Greek claims, by stressing what repute
The Persian monarch and the Persian nation
Won by this salutary demonstration:
Despite a strong defence and adverse weather
All arms combined magnificently together.

1805

At Viscount Nelson's lavish funeral,
    While the mob milled and yelled about St Paul's,
A General chatted with an Admiral:

'One of your Colleagues, Sir, remarked today
    That Nelson's *exit*, though to be lamented,
Falls not inopportunely, in its way.'

'He was a thorn in our flesh,' came the reply –
    'The most bird-witted, unaccountable,
Odd little runt that ever I did spy.

'One arm, one peeper, vain as Pretty Poll,
    A meddler, too, in foreign politics
And gave his heart in pawn to a plain moll.

'He would dare lecture us Sea Lords, and then
    Would treat his ratings as though men of honour
And play at leap-frog with his midshipmen!

'We tried to box him down, but up he popped,
    And when he'd banged Napoleon at the Nile
Became too much the hero to be dropped.

'You've heard that Copenhagen "blind eye" story?
    We'd tied him to Nurse Parker's apron-strings –
By G–d, he snipped them through and snatched the
        glory!'

'Yet,' cried the General, 'six-and-twenty sail
    Captured or sunk by him off Tráfalgár –
That writes a handsome *finis* to the tale.'

[77]

'Handsome enough. The seas are England's now.
   That fellow's foibles need no longer plague us.
He died most creditably, I'll allow.'

'And, Sir, the secret of his victories?'
   'By his unServicelike, familiar ways, Sir,
He made the whole Fleet love him, damn his eyes!'

The Last Day of Leave

(1916)

We five looked out over the moor
At rough hills blurred with haze, and a still sea:
Our tragic day, bountiful from the first.

We would spend it by the lily lake
(High in a fold beyond the farthest ridge),
Following the cart-track till it faded out.

The time of berries and bell-heather;
Yet all that morning nobody went by
But shepherds and one old man carting turfs.

We were in love: he with her, she with him,
And I, the youngest one, the odd man out,
As deep in love with a yet nameless muse.

No cloud; larks and heath-butterflies,
And herons undisturbed fishing the streams;
A slow cool breeze that hardly stirred the grass.

When we hurried down the rocky slope,
A flock of ewes galloping off in terror,
There shone the waterlilies, yellow and white.

Deep water and a shelving bank.
Off went our clothes and in we went, all five,
Diving like trout between the lily groves.

The basket had been nobly filled:
Wine and fresh rolls, chicken and pineapple –
Our braggadocio under threat of war.

The fire on which we boiled our kettle
We fed with ling and rotten blackthorn root;
And the coffee tasted memorably of peat.

Two of us might stray off together
But never less than three kept by the fire,
Focus of our uncertain destinies.

We spoke little, our minds in tune –
A sigh or laugh would settle any theme;
The sun so hot it made the rocks quiver.

But when it rolled down level with us,
Four pairs of eyes sought mine as if appealing
For a blind-fate-aversive afterword: –

'Do you remember the lily lake?
We were all there, all five of us in love,
Not one yet killed, widowed or broken-hearted.'

Amergin's Charm

[The text restored from mediaeval Irish and Welsh variants.]

I am a stag: *of seven tines,*
I am a flood: *across a plain,*
I am a wind: *on a deep lake,*
I am a tear: *the Sun lets fall,*

[79]

I am a hawk: *above the cliff,*
I am a thorn: *beneath the nail,*
I am a wonder: *among flowers,*
I am a wizard: *who but I*
Sets the cool head aflame with smoke?

I am a spear: *that roars for blood,*
I am a salmon: *in a pool,*
I am a lure: *from paradise,*
I am a hill: *where poets walk,*
I am a boar: *renowned and red,*
I am a breaker: *threatening doom,*
I am a tide: *that drags to death,*
I am an infant: *who but I*
Peeps from the unhewn dolmen arch?

I am the womb: *of every holt,*
I am the blaze: *on every hill,*
I am the queen: *of every hive,*
I am the shield: *for every head,*
I am the grave: *of every hope.*

The Song of Blodeuwedd

[Text reassembled and restored from the same
poem-medley as the foregoing.]

Not of father nor of mother
Was my blood, was my body.
I was spellbound by Gwydion,
Prime enchanter of the Britons,
When he formed me from nine blossoms,
    Nine buds of various kind:
From primrose of the mountain,

Broom, meadow-sweet and cockle,
　　Together intertwined,
From the bean in its shade bearing
A white spectral army
　　Of earth, of earthy kind,
From blossoms of the nettle,
Oak, thorn and bashful chestnut –
Nine powers of nine flowers,
　　Nine powers in me combined,
　　　Nine buds of plant and tree.
Long and white are my fingers
　　As the ninth wave of the sea.

Intercession in Late October

How hard the year dies: no frost yet.
On drifts of yellow sand Midas reclines,
Fearless of moaning reed or sullen wave.
Firm and fragrant still the brambleberries.
On ivy-bloom butterflies wag.

Spare him a little longer, Crone,
For his clean hands and love-submissive heart.

The White Goddess

All saints revile her, and all sober men
Ruled by the God Apollo's golden mean –
In scorn of which we sailed to find her
In distant regions likeliest to hold her
Whom we desired above all things to know,
Sister of the mirage and echo.

It was a virtue not to stay,
To go our headstrong and heroic way
Seeking her out at the volcano's head,
Among pack ice, or where the track had faded
Beyond the cavern of the seven sleepers:
Whose broad high brow was white as any leper's,
Whose eyes were blue, with rowan-berry lips,
With hair curled honey-coloured to white hips.

Green sap of Spring in the young wood a-stir
Will celebrate the Mountain Mother,
And every song-bird shout awhile for her;
But we are gifted, even in November
Rawest of seasons, with so huge a sense
Of her nakedly worn magnificence
We forget cruelty and past betrayal,
Heedless of where the next bright bolt may fall.

Counting the Beats

You, love, and I,
(He whispers) you and I,
And if no more than only you and I
What care you or I?

Counting the beats,
Counting the slow heart beats,
The bleeding to death of time in slow heart beats,
Wakeful they lie.

Cloudless day,
Night, and a cloudless day,
Yet the huge storm will burst upon their heads
    one day
From a bitter sky.

Where shall we be,
(She whispers) where shall we be,
When death strikes home, O where then shall we be
Who were you and I?

Not there but here,
(He whispers) only here,
As we are, here, together, now and here,
Always you and I.

Counting the beats,
Counting the slow heart beats,
The bleeding to death of time in slow heart beats,
Wakeful they lie.

The Death Room

Look forward, truant, to your second childhood.
The crystal sphere discloses
Wall-paper roses mazily repeated
In pink and bronze, their bunches harbouring
Elusive faces, under an inconclusive
Circling, spidery, ceiling craquelure,
And, by the window-frame, the well-loathed, lame,
Damp-patch, cross-patch, sleepless L-for-Lemur
Who, puffed to giant size,
Waits jealously till children close their eyes.

My Name and I

The impartial Law enrolled a name
    For my especial use:
My rights in it would rest the same
Whether I puffed it into fame
    Or sank it in abuse.

[83]

Robert was what my parents guessed
　　When first they peered at me,
And *Graves* an honourable bequest
With Georgian silver and the rest
　　From my male ancestry.

They taught me: 'You are *Robert Graves*
　　(Which you must learn to spell),
But see that *Robert Graves* behaves,
Whether with honest men or knaves,
　　Exemplarily well.'

Then though my I was always I,
　　Illegal and unknown,
With nothing to arrest it by –
As will be obvious when I die
　　And *Robert Graves* lives on –

I cannot well repudiate
　　This noun, this natal star,
This gentlemanly self, this mate
So kindly forced on me by fate,
　　Time and the registrar;

And therefore hurry him ahead
　　As an ambassador
To fetch me home my beer and bread
Or commandeer the best green bed,
　　As he has done before.

Yet, understand, I am not he
　　Either in mind or limb;
My name will take less thought for me,
In worlds of men I cannot see,
　　Than ever I for him.

Darien

It is a poet's privilege and fate
To fall enamoured of the one Muse
Who variously haunts this island earth.

She was your mother, Darien,
And presaged by the darting halcyon bird
Would run green-sleeved along her ridges,
Treading the asphodels and heather-trees
With white feet bare.

Often at moonrise I had watched her go,
And a cold shudder shook me
To see the curved blaze of her Cretan axe.
Averted her set face, her business
Not yet with me, long-striding,
She would ascend the peak and pass from sight.
But once at full moon, by the sea's verge,
I came upon her without warning.

Unrayed she stood, with long hair streaming,
A cockle-shell cupped in her warm hands,
Her axe propped idly on a stone.

No awe possessed me, only a great grief;
Wanly she smiled, but would not lift her eyes
(As a young girl will greet the stranger).
I stood upright, a head taller than she.
'See who has come,' said I.

She answered: 'If I lift my eyes to yours
And our eyes marry, man, what then?
Will they engender my son Darien?
Swifter than wind, with straight and nut-brown hair,
Tall, slender-shanked, grey-eyed, untameable;

Never was born, nor ever will be born
A child to equal my son Darien,
Guardian of the hid treasures of your world.'

I knew then by the trembling of her hands
For whom that flawless blade would sweep:
My own oracular head, swung by its hair.

'Mistress,' I cried, 'the times are evil
And you have charged me with their remedy.
O, where my head is now, let nothing be
But a clay counterfeit with nacre blink:
Only look up, so Darien may be born!

'He is the northern star, the spell of knowledge,
Pride of all hunters and all fishermen,
Your deathless fawn, an eaglet of your eyrie,
The topmost branch of your unfellable tree,
A tear streaking the summer night,
The new green of my hope.'
                                              Lifting her eyes,
She held mine for a lost eternity.
'Sweetheart,' said I, 'strike now, for Darien's sake!'

The Survivor

To die with a forlorn hope, but soon to be raised
By hags, the spoilers of the field, to elude their claws
And stand once more on a well-swept parade-ground,
Scarred and bemedalled, sword upright in fist
At head of a new undaunted company:

Is this joy? – to be doubtless alive again,
And the others dead? Will your nostrils gladly savour
The fragrance, always new, of a first hedge-rose?

Will your ears be charmed by the thrush's melody
Sung as though he had himself devised it?

And is this joy: after the double suicide
(Heart against heart) to be restored entire,
To smooth your hair and wash away the life-blood,
And presently seek a young and innocent bride,
Whispering in the dark: 'for ever and ever'?

The Foreboding

Looking by chance in at the open window
    I saw my own self seated in his chair
With gaze abstracted, furrowed forehead,
    Unkempt hair.

I thought that I had suddenly come to die,
    That to a cold corpse this was my farewell,
Until the pen moved slowly upon paper
    And tears fell.

He had written a name, yours, in printed letters:
    One word on which bemusedly to pore –
No protest, no desire, your naked name,
    Nothing more.

Would it be tomorrow, would it be next year?
    But the vision was not false, this much I knew;
And I turned angrily from the open window
    Aghast at you.

Why never a warning, either by speech or look
    That the love you cruelly gave me could not last?
Already it was too late: the bait swallowed,
    The hook fast.

The Straw

Peace, the wild valley streaked with torrents,
A hoopoe perched on his warm rock. Then why
This tremor of the straw between my fingers?

What should I fear? Have I not testimony
In her own hand, signed with her own name
That my love fell as lightning on her heart?

These questions, bird, are not rhetorical.
Watch how the straw twitches and leaps
As though the earth quaked at a distance.

Requited love; but better unrequited
If this chance instrument gives warning
Of cataclysmic anguish far away.

Were she at ease, warmed by the thought of me,
Would not my hand stay steady as this rock?
Have I undone her by my vehemence?

Dialogue on the Headland

She: You'll not forget these rocks and what I told you?
He: How could I? Never: whatever happens.
She: What do you think might happen?
    Might you fall out of love? – did you mean that?
He: Never, never! 'Whatever' was a sop
    For jealous listeners in the shadows.
She: You haven't answered me. I asked:
    'What do you think might happen?'

He: Whatever happens: though the skies should fall
       Raining their larks and vultures in our laps –
She: 'Though the seas turn to slime' – say that –
       'Though water-snakes be hatched with six heads.'
He: Though the seas turn to slime, or tower
       In an arching wave above us, three miles high –
She: 'Though she should break with you' – dare you say
         that?
       'Though she deny her words on oath.'
He: I had that in my mind to say, or nearly;
       It hurt so much I choked it back.
She: How many other days can't you forget?
       How many other loves and landscapes?
He: You are jealous?
She: Damnably.
He: The past is past.
She: And this?
He: Whatever happens, this goes on.
She: Without a future? Sweetheart, tell me now:
       What do you want of me? I must know that.
He: Nothing that isn't freely mine already.
She: Say what is freely yours and you shall have it.
He: Nothing that, loving you, I could dare take.
She: O, for an answer with no 'nothing' in it!
He: Then give me everything that's left.
She: Left after what?
He: After whatever happens:
       Skies have already fallen, seas are slime,
       Watersnakes poke and peer six-headedly –
She: And I lie snugly in the Devil's arms.
He: I said: 'Whatever happens.' Are you crying?
She: You'll not forget me – ever, ever, ever?

Lovers in Winter

The posture of the tree
   Shows the prevailing wind;
And ours, long misery
   When you are long unkind.

But forward, look, we lean –
   Not backward as in doubt –
And still with branches green
   Ride our ill weather out.

The Sea Horse

Since now in every public place
Lurk phantoms who assume your walk and face,
You cannot yet have utterly abjured me
Nor stifled the insistent roar of sea.

Do as I do: confide your unquiet love
(For one who never owed you less than love)
To this indomitable hippocamp,
Child of your element, coiled a-ramp,
Having ridden out worse tempests than you know of;
Under his horny ribs a blood-red stain
Portends renewal of our pain.
Sweetheart, make much of him and shed
Tears on his taciturn dry head.

Cat-Goddesses

A perverse habit of cat-goddesses –
Even the blackest of them, black as coals
Save for a new moon blazing on each breast,
With coral tongues and beryl eyes like lamps,
Long-leggèd, pacing three by three in nines –
This obstinate habit is to yield themselves,
In verisimilar love-ecstasies,
To tatter-eared and slinking alley-toms
No less below the common run of cats
Than they above it; which they do for spite,
To provoke jealousy – not the least abashed
By such gross-headed, rabbit-coloured litters
As soon they shall be happy to desert.

The Blue-Fly

Five summer days, five summer nights,
The ignorant, loutish, giddy blue-fly
Hung without motion on the cling peach,
Humming occasionally: 'O my love, my fair one!'
    As in the *Canticles*.

Magnified one thousand times, the insect
Looks farcically human; laugh if you will!
Bald head, stage-fairy wings, blear eyes,
A caved-in chest, hairy black mandibles,
    Long spindly thighs.

The crime was detected on the sixth day.
What then could be said or done? By anyone?
It would have been vindictive, mean and what-not
To swat that fly for being a blue-fly,
    For debauch of a peach.

Is it fair, either, to bring a microscope
To bear on the case, even in search of truth?
Nature, doubtless, has some compelling cause
To glut the carriers of her epidemics –
    Nor did the peach complain.

Rhea

On her shut lids the lightning flickers,
Thunder explodes above her bed,
An inch from her lax arm the rain hisses;
Discrete she lies,

Not dead but entranced, dreamlessly
With slow breathing, her lips curved
In a half-smile archaic, her breast bare,
Hair astream.

The house rocks, a flood suddenly rising
Bears away bridges: oak and ash
Are shivered to the roots – royal green timber.
She nothing cares.

(Divine Augustus, trembling at the storm,
Wrapped sealskin on his thumb; divine Gaius
Made haste to hide himself in a deep cellar,
Distraught by fear.)

Rain, thunder, lightning: pretty children.
'Let them play,' her mother-mind repeats;
'They do no harm, unless from high spirits
Or by mishap.'

With Her Lips Only

This honest wife, challenged at dusk
At the garden gate, under a moon perhaps,
In scent of honeysuckle, dared to deny
Love to an urgent lover: with her lips only,
Not with her heart. It was no assignation;
Taken aback, what could she say else?
For the children's sake, the lie was venial;
'For the children's sake', she argued with her conscience.

Yet a mortal lie must follow before dawn:
Challenged as usual in her own bed,
She protests love to an urgent husband,
Not with her heart but with her lips only;
'For the children's sake', she argues with her conscience.
'For the children' – turning suddenly cold towards them.

Penthesileia

Penthesileia, dead of profuse wounds,
Was despoiled of her arms by Prince Achilles
Who, for love of that fierce white naked corpse,
Necrophily on her committed
In the public view.

Some gasped, some groaned, some bawled their
     indignation,
Achilles nothing cared, distraught by grief,
But suddenly caught Thersites' obscene snigger
And with one vengeful buffet to the jaw
Dashed out his life.

This was a fury few might understand,
Yet Penthesileia, hailed by Prince Achilles
On the Elysian plain, pauses to thank him
For avenging her insulted womanhood
With sacrifice.

Spoils

When all is over and you march for home,
The spoils of war are easily disposed of:
Standards, weapons of combat, helmets, drums
May decorate a staircase or a study,
While lesser gleanings of the battlefield –
Coins, watches, wedding-rings, gold teeth and such –
Are sold anonymously for solid cash.

The spoils of love present a different case,
When all is over and you march for home:
That lock of hair, these letters and the portrait
May not be publicly displayed; nor sold;
Nor burned; nor returned (the heart being obstinate) –
Yet never dare entrust them to a safe
For fear they burn a hole through two-foot steel.

The Face in the Mirror

Grey haunted eyes, absent-mindedly glaring
From wide, uneven orbits; one brow drooping
Somewhat over the eye
Because of a missile fragment still inhering,
Skin deep, as a foolish record of old-world fighting.

[94]

Crookedly broken nose – low tackling caused it;
Cheeks, furrowed; coarse grey hair, flying frenetic;
Forehead, wrinkled and high;
Jowls, prominent; ears, large; jaw, pugilistic;
Teeth, few; lips, full and ruddy; mouth, ascetic.

I pause with razor poised, scowling derision
At the mirrored man whose beard needs my attention,
And once more ask him why
He still stands ready, with a boy's presumption,
To court the queen in her high silk pavilion.

The Naked and the Nude

For me, the naked and the nude
(By lexicographers construed
As synonyms that should express
The same deficiency of dress
Or shelter) stand as wide apart
As love from lies, or truth from art.

Lovers without reproach will gaze
On bodies naked and ablaze;
The Hippocratic eye will see
In nakedness, anatomy;
And naked shines the Goddess when
She mounts her lion among men.

The nude are bold, the nude are sly
To hold each treasonable eye.
While draping by a showman's trick
Their dishabille in rhetoric,
They grin a mock-religious grin
Of scorn at those of naked skin.

The naked, therefore, who compete
Against the nude may know defeat;
Yet when they both together tread
The briary pastures of the dead,
By Gorgons with long whips pursued,
How naked go the sometime nude!

Woman and Tree

To love one woman, or to sit
    Always beneath the same tall tree,
Argues a certain lack of wit
    Two steps from imbecility.

A poet, therefore, sworn to feed
    On every food the senses know,
Will claim the inexorable need
    To be Don Juan Tenorio.

Yet if, miraculously enough,
    (And why set miracles apart?)
Woman and tree prove of a stuff
    Wholly to glamour his wild heart?

And if such visions from the void
    As shone in fever there, or there,
Assemble, hold and are enjoyed
    On climbing one familiar stair . . . ?

To change and chance he took a vow,
    As he thought fitting. None the less,
What of a phoenix on the bough,
    Or a sole woman's fatefulness?

The Second-Fated

My stutter, my cough, my unfinished sentences,
Denote an inveterate physical reluctance
To use the metaphysical idiom.
Forgive me: what I am saying is, perhaps this: –

Your accepted universe, by Jove's naked hand
Or Esmun's, or Odomankoma's, or Marduk's –
Choose which name jibes – formed scientifically
From whatever there was before Time was,
And begging the question of perfect consequence,
May satisfy the general run of men
(If 'run' be an apt term for patent paralytics)
That blueprints destine all they suffer here,
But does not satisfy certain few else.

Fortune enrolled me among the second-fated
Who have read their own obituaries in *The Times*,
Have heard 'Where, death, thy sting? Where, grave,
    thy victory?'
Intoned with unction over their still clay,
Have seen two parallel red-ink lines drawn
Under their manic-depressive bank accounts,
And are therefore strictly forbidden to walk in
    grave-yards
Lest they scandalize the sexton and his bride.

We, to be plain with you, taking advantage
Of a brief demise, visited first the Pit,
A library of shades, completed characters;
And next the silver-bright Hyperborean Queendom,
Basking under the sceptre of Guess Whom?
Where pure souls matrilineally foregather.
We were then shot through by merciful lunar shafts

Until hearts tingled, heads sang, and praises flowed;
And learned to scorn your factitious universe
Ruled by the death which we had flouted;
Acknowledging only that from the Dove's egg hatched
Before aught was, but wind – unpredictable
As our second birth would be, or our second love:
A moon-warmed world of discontinuance.

A Slice of Wedding Cake

Why have such scores of lovely, gifted girls
    Married impossible men?
Simple self-sacrifice may be ruled out,
    And missionary endeavour, nine times out of ten.

Repeat 'impossible men': not merely rustic,
    Foul-tempered or depraved
(Dramatic foils chosen to show the world
    How well women behave, and always have behaved).

Impossible men: idle, illiterate,
    Self-pitying, dirty, sly,
For whose appearance even in City parks
    Excuses must be made to casual passers-by.

Has God's supply of tolerable husbands
    Fallen, in fact, so low?
Or do I always over-value woman
    At the expense of man?
                    Do I?
                            It might be so.

Call It a Good Marriage

Call it a good marriage –
For no one ever questioned
Her warmth, his masculinity,
Their interlocking views;
Except one stray graphologist
Who frowned in speculation
At her h's and her s's,
His p's and w's.

Though few would still subscribe
To the monogamic axiom
That strife below the hip-bones
Need not estrange the heart,
Call it a good marriage:
More drew those two together,
Despite a lack of children,
Than pulled them apart.

Call it a good marriage:
They never fought in public,
They acted circumspectly
And faced the world with pride;
Thus the hazards of their love-bed
Were none of our damned business –
Till as jurymen we sat upon
Two deaths by suicide.

The Twin of Sleep

Death is the twin of Sleep, they say:
  For I shall rise renewed,
Free from the cramps of yesterday,
  Clear-eyed and supple-thewed.

But though this bland analogy
    Helps other folk to face
Decrepitude, senility,
    Madness, disease, disgrace,

I do not like Death's greedy looks:
    Give me his twin instead –
Sleep never auctions off my books,
    My boots, my shirts, my bed.

Around the Mountain

Some of you may know, others perhaps can guess
    How it is to walk all night through summer rain
(Thin rain that shrouds a beneficent full moon),
    To circle a mountain, and then limp home again.

The experience varies with a traveller's age
    And bodily strength, and strength of the love affair
That harries him out of doors in steady drizzle,
    With neither jacket nor hat, and holds him there.

Still, let us concede some common elements:
    Wild-fire that, until midnight, burns his feet;
And surging rankly up, strong on the palate,
    Scents of July, imprisoned by long heat.

Add: the sub-human, black tree-silhouettes
    Against a featureless pale pall of sky;
Unseen, gurgling water; the bulk and menace
    Of entranced houses; a wraith wandering by.

Milestones, each one witness of a new mood –
    Anger, desperation, grief, regret;
Her too-familiar face that whirls and totters
    In memory, never willing to stay set.

Whoever makes the desired turning-point,
  Which means another fifteen miles to go,
Learns more from dawn than love, so far, has taught him:
  Especially the false dawn, when cocks first crow.

Those last few miles are easy: being assured
  Of the truth, why should he fabricate fresh lies?
His house looms up; the eaves drip drowsily;
  The windows blaze to a resolute sunrise.

Symptoms of Love

Love is a universal migraine,
A bright stain on the vision
Blotting out reason.

Symptoms of true love
Are leanness, jealousy,
Laggard dawns;

Are omens and nightmares –
Listening for a knock,
Waiting for a sign:

For a touch of her fingers
In a darkened room,
For a searching look.

Take courage, lover!
Could you endure such grief
At any hand but hers?

Under the Olives

We never would have loved had love not struck
Swifter than reason, and despite reason:
Under the olives, our hands interlocked,
We both fell silent:
Each listened for the other's answering
Sigh of unreasonableness –
Innocent, gentle, bold, enduring, proud.

The Starred Coverlet

A difficult achievement for true lovers
Is to lie mute, without embrace or kiss,
Without a rustle or a smothered sigh,
Basking each in the other's glory.

Let us not undervalue lips or arms
As reassurances of constancy,
Or speech as necessary communication
When troubled hearts go groping through the dusk;

Yet lovers who have learned this last refinement –
To lie apart, yet sleep and dream together
Motionless under their starred coverlet –
Crown love with wreaths of myrtle.

Hag-Ridden

I awoke in profuse sweat, arms aching,
Knees bruised and soles cut to the raw –
Preserved no memory of that night
But whipcracks and my own voice screaming.

Through what wild, flinty wastes of fury,
Hag of the Mill,
Did you ride your madman?

Turn of the Moon

Never forget who brings the rain
In swarthy goatskin bags from a far sea:
It is the Moon as she turns, repairing
Damages of long drought and sunstroke.

Never count upon rain, never foretell it,
For no power can bring rain
Except the Moon as she turns; and who can rule her?

She is prone to delay the necessary floods,
Lest such a gift might become obligation,
A month, or two, or three; then suddenly
Not relenting but by way of whim
Will perhaps conjure from the cloudless west
A single rain-drop to surprise with hope
Each haggard, upturned face.

Were the Moon a Sun, we would count upon her
To bring rain seasonably as she turned;
Yet no one thinks to thank the regular Sun
For shining fierce in summer, mild in winter –
Why should the Moon so drudge?

But if one night she brings us, as she turns,
Soft, steady, even, copious rain
That harms no leaf nor flower, but gently falls
Hour after hour, sinking to the tap roots,
And the sodden earth exhales at dawn
A long sigh scented with pure gratitude,

Such rain – the first rain of our lives, it seems,
Neither foretold, cajoled, nor counted on –
Is woman giving as she loves.

The Miller's Man

The imperturbable miller's man
Whose help the boy implored, drowning,
Drifting slowly past the mill,
Was a stout swimmer, yet would not come between
The river-god and his assured victim.

Soon he, too, swimming in the sun,
Is caught with cramp; and the boy's ghost
Jeers from the reeds and rushes.
But he drowns valiantly in silence,
This being no one's business but his own.

Let us not reckon the miller's man
With Judas or with Jesus,
But with the cattle, who endure all weathers,
Or with the mill-wheel foolishly creaking,
Incurious of the grain in the bins.

The Broken Girth

Bravely from Fairyland he rode, on furlough,
Astride a tall bay given him by the Queen
From whose couch he had leaped not a half-hour since,
Whose lilies-of-the-valley shone from his helm.

But alas, as he paused to assist five Ulstermen
Sweating to raise a recumbent Ogham pillar,
Breach of a saddle-girth tumbled Oisín

To common Irish earth. And at once, it is said,
Old age came on him with grief and frailty.

St Patrick asked: would he not confess the Christ? –
Which for that Lady's sake he loathed to do,
But northward loyally turned his eyes in death.
It was Fenians bore the unshriven corpse away
For burial, keening.
                    Curse me all squint-eyed monks
Who misconstrue the passing of Finn's son:
Old age, not Fairyland, was his delusion.

Hedges Freaked with Snow

(Song for the Lute III)

No argument, no anger, no remorse,
    No dividing of blame.
There was poison in the cup – why should we ask
    From whose hand it came?

No grief for our dead love, no howling gales
    That through darkness blow,
But the smile of sorrow, a wan winter landscape,
    Hedges freaked with snow.

At Best, Poets

Woman with her forests, moons, flowers, waters,
And watchful fingers:
We claim no magic comparable to hers –
At best, poets; at worst, sorcerers.

A Last Poem

A last poem, and a very last, and yet another –
O, when can I give over?
Must I drive the pen until blood bursts from my nails
And my breath fails and I shake with fever,
Or sit well wrapped in a many-coloured cloak
Where the moon shines new through Castle Crystal?
Shall I never hear her whisper softly:
'But this is truth written by you only,
And for me only; therefore, love, have done'?

Judgement of Paris

What if Prince Paris, after taking thought,
Had not adjudged the apple to Aphrodite
But, instead, had favoured buxom Hera,
Divine defendress of the marriage couch?
What if Queen Helen had been left to squander
Her beauty upon the thralls of Menelaus,
Hector to die unhonoured in his bed,
Penthesileia to hunt a poorer quarry,
The bards to celebrate a meaner siege?
Could we still have found the courage, you and I,
To embark together for Cranaë
And consummate our no less fateful love?

The Three-Faced

Who calls her two-faced? Faces, she has three:
The first inscrutable, for the outer world;
The second shrouded in self-contemplation;
The third, her face of love,
Once for an endless moment turned on me.

Dance of Words

To make them move, you should start from lightning
And not forecast the rhythm: rely on chance,
Or so-called chance for its bright emergence
Once lightning interpenetrates the dance.

Grant them their own traditional steps and postures
But see they dance it out again and again
Until only lightning is left to puzzle over –
The choreography plain, and the theme plain.

The Oleaster

Each night for seven nights beyond the gulf
A storm raged, out of hearing, and crooked flashes
Of lightning animated us. Before day-break
Rain fell munificently for the earth's need. . .

No, here they never plant the sweet olive
As some do (bedding slips in a prepared trench),
But graft it on the club of Hercules
The savage, inexpugnable oleaster
Whose roots and bole bunching from limestone
    crannies
Sprout impudent shoots born only to be lopped
Spring after Spring. Theirs is a loveless berry. . .

By mid-day we walk out, with naked feet,
Through pools on the road, gazing at waterfalls
Or a line of surf, but mostly at the trees
Whose elegant branches rain has duly blackened
And pressed their crowns to a sparkling silver.

Innumerable, plump with promise of oil,
The olives hang grass-green, in thankfulness
For a bitter sap and bitter New Year snows
That cleansed their bark. . .

                  Forgive me, dearest love,
If nothing I can say be strange or new.
I am no child of the hot South like you,
Though in rock rooted like an oleaster.

A Measure of Casualness

Too fierce the candlelight; your gentle voice
Roars as in dream: my shoulder-nooks flower;
A scent of honeysuckle invades the house,
And my fingertips are so love-enhanced
That sailcloth feels like satin to them.
Teach me a measure of casualness
Though you stalk into my room like Venus naked.

Not to Sleep

Not to sleep all the night long, for pure joy,
Counting no sheep and careless of chimes,
Welcoming the dawn confabulation
Of birds, her children, who discuss idly
Fanciful details of the promised coming –
Will she be wearing red, or russet, or blue,
Or pure white? – whatever she wears, glorious:

Not to sleep all the night long, for pure joy,
This is given to few but at last to me,
So that when I laugh and stretch and leap from bed

I shall glide downstairs, my feet brushing the carpet
In courtesy to civilized progression,
Though, did I wish, I could soar through the open
    window
And perch on a branch above, acceptable ally
Of the birds still alert, grumbling gently together.

Black

Black drinks the sun and draws all colours to it.
I am bleached white, my truant love. Come back,
And stain me with intensity of black.

Good Night to the Old Gods

Good night, old gods, all this long year so faint
You propped your heavy eyelids up with shells!
Though once we honoured you who ruled this land
One hundred generations and ten more,
Our mood has changed: you dribble at the mouth,
Your dark-blue fern-tattoos are faded green,
Your thunderous anger wanes to petulance,
And love to groanings of indifference.
What most you crave is rest in a rock-cave,
Seasonally aroused by raucous gulls
Or swallows, nodding off once more to sleep.

We lay you in a row with cool palm wine
Close at your elbows, should you suffer thirst,
And breadfruit piled on rushes by your feet;
But will not furnish you a standing guard –
We have fish to net and spear, taro to hoe,
Pigs to fatten, coco-trees to climb;

Nor are our poets so bedulled in spirit
They would mount a platform, praising in worn verse
Those fusillades of lightning hurled by you
At giants in a first day-break of time:
Whom you disarmed and stretched in a rock-cave
Not unlike this – you have forgotten where.

The Sweet-Shop Round the Corner

The child dreaming along a crowded street
Lost hold of his mother, who had turned to greet
Some neighbour, and mistakenly matched his tread
With a strange woman's. 'Buy me sweets,' he said,
Waving his hand, which he found warmly pressed;
So dragged her on, boisterous and self-possessed:
'The sweet-shop's round the corner!' Both went in,
And not for a long while did the child begin
To feel a dread that something had gone wrong:
Were Mother's legs so lean, or her shoes so long,
Or her skirt so patched, or her hair tousled and grey?
Why did she twitter in such a ghostly way?
'O Mother, are you dead?'
                              What else could a child say?

Bower-Bird

The Bower-bird improvised a cool retreat
For the hen he honoured, doing his poor best
With parrot-plumage, orchids, bones and corals,
To engage her fancy.
                          But this was no nest . . .
So, though the Penguin dropped at his hen's feet

An oval stone to signal: 'be my bride',
And though the Jackdaw's nest was glorified
With diamond rings and brooches massed inside,
It was the Bower-bird who contented me
By not equating love with matrimony.

Bites and Kisses

Heather and holly,
Bites and kisses,
A courtship-royal
On the hill's red cusp.
Look up, look down,
Gaze all about you –
A livelier world
By ourselves contrived:

Swan in full course
Up the Milky Way,
Moon in her wildness,
Sun ascendant
In Crab or Lion,
Beyond the bay
A pride of dolphins
Curving and tumbling
With bites and kisses . . .

Or dog-rose petals
Well-starred by dew,
Or jewelled pebbles,
Or waterlilies open
For the dragon-flies
In their silver and blue.

A Bracelet

A bracelet invisible
For your busy wrist,
Twisted from silver
Spilt afar,
From silver of the clear Moon,
From her sheer halo,
From the male beauty
Of a shooting star.

Her Brief Withdrawal

'Forgive me, love, if I withdraw awhile:
It is only that you ask such bitter questions,
Always another beyond the extreme last.
And the answers astound: you have entangled me
In my own mystery. Grant me a respite:
I was happier far, not asking, nor much caring,
Choosing by appetite only: self-deposed,
Self-reinstated, no one observing.
When I belittled this vibrancy of touch
And the active vengeance of these folded arms
No one could certify my powers for me
Or my saining virtue, or know that I compressed
Knots of destiny in a careless fist,
I who had passed for a foundling from the hills
Of innocent and flower-like phantasies,
Though minting silver by my mere tread . . .
Did I not dote on you, I well might strike you
For implicating me in your true dream.'

At Seventy-Two

At seventy-two,
Being older than you,
I can rise when I please
Without slippers or shoes
And go down to the kitchen
To eat what I choose –
Jam, tomatoes and cheese –
Then I visit the garden
And wander at ease
Past the bed where what grows is
A huge clump of roses
And I swing in the swing
Set up under the trees
My mouth full of biscuits,
My hat on my knees.

Song: Dew-Drop and Diamond

The difference between you and her
(Whom I to you did once prefer)
Is clear enough to settle:
She like a diamond shone, but you
Shine like an early drop of dew
Poised on a red rose-petal.

The dew-drop carries in its eye
Mountain and forest, sea and sky,
With every change of weather;
Contrariwise, a diamond splits
The prospect into idle bits
That none can piece together.

The Home-Coming

At the tangled heart of a wood I fell asleep,
Bewildered by her silence and her absence –
As though such potent lulls in love were not
Ordained by the demands of pure music.

A bird sang: 'Close your eyes, it is not for long –
Dream of what gold and crimson she will wear
In honour of your oak-brown.'

It was her hoopoe. Yet, when the spread heavens
Of my feast night glistened with shooting stars
And she walked unheralded up through the dim light
Of the home lane, I did not recognise her –
So lost a man can be
Who feeds on hopes and fears and memory.

Wigs and Beards

In the bad old days a bewigged country Squire
Would never pay his debts, unless at cards,
Shot, angled, urged his pack through standing grain,
Horsewhipped his tenantry, snorted at the arts,
Toped himself under the table every night,
Blasphemed God with a cropful of God-damns,
Aired whorehouse French or lame Italian,
Set fashions of pluperfect slovenliness
And claimed seigneurial rights over all women
Who slept, imprudently, under the same roof.

Taxes and wars long ago ploughed them under –
'And serve the bastards right' the Beards agree,
Hurling their empties through the café window
And belching loud as they proceed downstairs.
Latter-day bastards of that famous stock,
They never rode a nag, nor gaffed a trout,
Nor winged a pheasant, nor went soldiering,
But remain true to the same hell-fire code
In all available particulars
And scorn to pay their debts even at cards.
Moreunder (which is to subtract, not add),
Their ancestors called themselves gentlemen
As they, in the same sense, call themselves artists.

Astymelusa

'Astymelusa!'
        Knees at your approach
Suddenly give, more than in sleep or death –
As well they may; such love compels them.
'Astymelusa!'
        But no answer comes.
Crowned with a leafy crown, the girl passes
Like a star afloat through glittering sky,
Or a golden flower, or drifted thistledown.

* A fragment by the Dorian Greek poet Alcman, seventh
century B.C., found among the Oxyrhynchus papyri.

The Yet Unsayable

It was always fiercer, brighter, gentler than could be told
Even in words quickened by Truth's dark eye:
Its absence, whirlpool; its presence, deluge;
Its time, astonishment; its magnitude,
A murderous dagger-point.
                    So we surrender
Our voices to the dried and scurrying leaves
And choose our own long-predetermined path
From the unsaid to the yet unsayable
In silence of love and love's temerity.

The Narrow Sea

With you for mast and sail and flag,
And anchor never known to drag,
Death's narrow but oppressive sea
Looks not unnavigable to me.

The Olive-Yard

Now by a sudden shift of eye
The hitherto exemplary world
Takes on immediate wildness
And birds, trees, winds, the very letters
Of our childhood's alphabet, alter
Into rainbowed mysteries.

Flesh is no longer flesh, but power;
Numbers, no longer arithmetical,
Dance like lambs, fly like doves;

And silence falls at last, though silken branches
Gently heave in the near olive-yard
And vague cloud labours on.

Whose was the stroke of summer genius
Flung from a mountain fastness
Where the griffon-vulture soars
That let us read our shrouded future
As easily as a book of prayer
Spread open on the knee?

Poisoned Day

The clouds dripped poisonous dew to spite
A day for weeks looked forward to. True love
Sickened that evening without remedy:
We neither quarrelled, kissed, nor said good-night
But fell asleep, our arms around each other,
And awoke to the gentle hiss of rain on grass
And thrushes calling that the worst was over.

Armistice Day, 1918

What's all this hubbub and yelling,
   Commotion and scamper of feet,
With ear-splitting clatter of kettles and cans,
   Wild laughter down Mafeking Street?

O, those are the kids whom we fought for
   (You might think they'd been scoffing our rum)
With flags that they waved when we marched off to war
   In the rapture of bugle and drum.

Now they'll hang Kaiser Bill from a lamp-post,
  Von Tirpitz they'll hang from a tree. . .
We've been promised a 'Land Fit for Heroes' –
  What heroes we heroes must be!

And the guns that we took from the Fritzes,
  That we paid for with rivers of blood,
Look, they're hauling them down to Old Battersea Bridge
  Where they'll topple them, souse, in the mud!

But there's old men and women in corners
  With tears falling fast on their cheeks,
There's the armless and legless and sightless –
  It's seldom that one of them speaks.

And there's flappers gone drunk and indecent,
  Their skirts kilted up to the thigh,
The constables lifting no hand in reproof
  And the chaplain averting his eye. . .

When the days of rejoicing are over,
  When the flags are stowed safely away,
They will dream of another wild 'War to End Wars'
  And another wild Armistice day.

But the boys who were killed in the trenches,
  Who fought with no rage and no rant,
We left them stretched out on their pallets of mud
  Low down with the worm and the ant.

The Judges

  Crouched on wet shingle at the cove
  In day-long search for treasure-trove –
  Meaning the loveliest-patterned pebble,

Of any colour imaginable,
Ground and smoothed by a gentle sea –
How seldom, Julia, we agree
On our day's find: the perfect one
To fetch back home when day is done,
Splendid enough to stupefy
The fiercest, most fastidious eye –
Tossing which back we tell the sea:
'Work on it one more century!'

My Ghost

I held a poor opinion of myself
When young, but never bettered my opinion
(Even by comparison)
Of all my fellow-fools at school or college.

Passage of years induced a tolerance,
Even a near-affection, for myself –
Which, when you fell in love with me, amounted
(Though with my tongue kept resolutely tied)
To little short of pride.

Pride brought its punishment: thus to be haunted
By my own ghost whom, much to my disquiet,
All would-be friends and open enemies
Boldly identified and certified
As me, including him in anecdotal
Autobiographies.

Love, should you meet him in the newspapers
In planes, on trains, or at large get-togethers,
I charge you, disregard his foolish capers;
Silence him with a cold unwinking stare

Where he sits opposite you at table
And let all present watch amazed, remarking
On how little you care.

The Green-Sailed Vessel

We are like doves, well-paired,
Veering across a meadow –
Children's voices below,
Their song and echo;

Like raven, wren or crow
That cry and prophesy,
What do we not foreknow,
Whether deep or shallow?

Like the tiller and prow
Of a green-sailed vessel
Voyaging, none knows how,
Between moon and shadow;

Like the restless, endless
Blossoming of a bough,
Like tansy, violet, mallow,
Like the sun's afterglow.

Of sharp resemblances
What further must I show
Until your black eyes narrow,
Furrowing your clear brow?

The Title of Poet

Poets are guardians
Of a shadowy island
With granges and forests
Warmed by the Moon.

Come back, child, come back!
You have been far away,
Housed among phantoms,
Reserving silence.

Whoever loves a poet
Continues whole-hearted,
Her other loves or loyalties
Distinct and clear.

She is young, he is old
And endures for her sake
Such fears of unease
As distance provokes.

Yet how can he warn her
What natural disasters
Will plague one who dares
To neglect her poet? . . .
For the title of poet
Comes only with death.

Pity

Sickness may seem a falling out of love,
With pleas for pity – love's lean deputy.
If so, refuse me pity, wait, love on:
Never outlaw me while I yet live.

The day may come when you too, falling sick,
Implore my pity. Let me, too, refuse it
Offering you, instead, my pitiless love.

Beatrice and Dante

He, a grave poet, fell in love with her.
She, a mere child, fell deep in love with love
And, being a child, illumined his whole heart.

From her clear conspect rose a whispering
With no hard words in innocency held back –
Until the day that she became woman,

Frowning to find her love imposed upon:
A new world beaten out in her own image –
For his own deathless glory.

Tilth

('Robert Graves, the British veteran, is no longer in the poetic swim.
He still resorts to traditional metres and rhyme, and to such
out-dated words as *tilth*; withholding his 100% approbation also
from contemporary poems that favour sexual freedom.'
From a New York critical weekly)

Gone are the drab monosyllabic days
When 'agricultural labour' still was *tilth*;
And '100% approbation', *praise*;
And 'pornographic modernism', *filth* –
Yet still I stand by *tilth* and *filth* and *praise*.

A Dream of Frances Speedwell

I fell in love at my first evening party.
You were tall and fair, just seventeen perhaps,
Talking to my two sisters. I kept silent
And never since have loved a tall fair girl,
Until last night in the small windy hours
When, floating up an unfamiliar staircase
And into someone's bedroom, there I found her
Posted beside the window in half-light
Wearing that same white dress with lacy sleeves.
She beckoned. I came closer. We embraced
Inseparably until the dream faded.
Her eyes shone clear and blue. . .

Who was it, though, impersonated you?

At the Gate

Where are poems? Why do I now write none?
This can mean no lack of pens, nor lack of love,
But need perhaps of an increased magic –
Where have my ancient powers suddenly gone?

Tonight I caught a glimpse of her at the gate
Grappling a monster never found before,
And jerking back its head. Had I come too late?
Her eyes blazed fire and I could look no more.

What could she hold against me? Never yet
Had I lied to her or thwarted her desire,
Rejecting prayers that I could never forget,
Stealing green leaves to light an alien fire.

Crucibles of Love

From where do poems come?
From workshops of the mind,
As do destructive armaments,
Philosophic calculations,
Schemes for man's betterment?

Or are poems born simply
From crucibles of love?
May not you and I together
Engrossed with each other
Assess their longevity?

For who else can judge merits
Or define demerits –
This remains a task for lovers
Held fast in love together
And for no others.

Three Times in Love

You have now fallen three times in love
With the same woman, first indeed blindly
And at her blind insistence;

Next with your heart alive to the danger
Of what hers might conceal, although such passion
Strikes nobly and for ever;

Now at last, deep in dream, transported
To her rose garden on the high ridge,
Assured that there she can deny you
No deserved privilege,
However controvertible or new.

Index of Titles and First Lines

[127]

[133]